What's Wrong with MICROSOFT Windows, Word and MSN

What's Wrong with MICROSOFT Windows, Word and MSN

Derek Kelly, Ph.D.

Authors Choice Press
San Jose New York Lincoln Shanghai

**What's Wrong with
MICROSOFT
Windows, Word and MSN**

Authors Choice Press
an imprint of iUniverse.com, Inc.

For information address:
iUniverse.com, Inc.
5220 S 16th, Ste. 200
Lincoln, NE 68512
www.iuniverse.com

ISBN: 0-595-20188-1

Printed in the United States of America

This one is for Ernie Perry

Contents

Preface

In 1978, spurred on by a life-long fascination with technology, I looked through the literature associated with at least ten different personal computers (Osborne, Cromenco, and Apple among them), then plunked down around $1000.00 and took home an Apple II computer (number 272 I think it was)—and my life has never been the same since.

Human-centered Computing

At the time, I was enthralled by the dreams of people like Steve Jobs and Ted Nelson who wanted to democratize the computer so that everyone on the planet could enjoy the benefits of computing power. Now, less than twenty-five years later the types of personal computers have dwindled to two (IBM PC and Apple Mac), and the number of people worldwide using personal computers must be close to or over a billion.

Similarly, operating systems of personal computers were many when the revolution first began, but now there are only three principal operating systems—from Apple, Microsoft, and Unix. While Apple continues to hold a share of the market, and while Unix-related operating systems, such as Linux, attempt to make some headway, the majority of users run the Microsoft Windows operating system on IBM-type personal computers. Without taking away anything from Apple or Unix, Microsoft's Windows is the dominant operating system in the world today, and most of the software running on personal computers runs "under" Microsoft Windows. This is true not only in the world of stand-alone systems, but in the Internet-connected world as well.

Along with the dreams of democratizing the computer, other dreams (in fact requirements) emerged over the years. These dreams focused on making the personal computer accessible to everyone, easy to understand and use, and a boon to productivity and creativity. But while the personal computer has become widespread and at least half a billion people are computing off or "on the Web" through personal computers and other related devices, how have the dreams of accessibility and ease of use fared?

Not so well, I'm afraid. Though every software development company in the market repeats the mantra of "user-friendliness" and of "human-centered" design few, if any, manage to achieve it. At least one recent writer[1] has argued that one reason why this aim has not been achieved is that our technology is not sufficiently advanced for we lack such things as natural language interfaces to computers. My view is slightly different from this. I think the reason we lack human-centered software is that the software is badly designed to begin with, and bad design will plague natural language interfaces or whatever other improvements we make in the future. Human-centered computing thus awaits better design, better architecture—not necessarily better technology.

---

1   See Michael Dertouzos, *The Unfinished Revolution: Human-Centered Computers and What they can do for Us*, Harper Collins Publishers, 2001.

Aim of the Book

In this book, I shall attempt to demonstrate that the reason why
we have not achieved the goal of user-friendly, human-centered
computing is that the design and implementation of the user
interface is poverty-stricken. I have elected to examine Microsoft
software (including the Windows operating system) in this book
because Microsoft is the dominant personal computer software
provider in the world.[2]

Flow of Work

There have been many studies of how users interact with computers. Just about every major software developer has a crew of
human factors experts who regularly either are involved in the
design of software or else perform tests after the fact on that software. The aim of these human factors personnel is to understand
the cognitive interaction of users with software, and help make
the interaction natural or intuitive.

This book is a sort of human factors study. While I am certainly concerned with the cognitive provisions and deficiencies
of Microsoft software generally, I am primarily concerned with
the way Microsoft software provides tools for the user in the
context of the flow of work. I want to examine what one can do
with these Microsoft products while following a process, a flow
of activities, to achieve some end.

---

2   While Microsoft is the largest PC software provider in the world, IBM is
    the largest software provider for all types of computers.

All work has an intention or aim. All work involves following a procedure to attain that aim. A procedure is a series of steps that flow from the start of a piece of work to the end or intention of that piece of work. All work is thus like a manufacturing process. Work flows from step to step. This is what I want to examine in this book. I want to examine what three computer programs provide as tools that allegedly can be used to perform work tasks. I want to determine what these products deliver to the flow of work.

Nature of the Critique

Instead of using a statistical sampling method, I shall, instead, use a method known as Phenomenology. This method begins and ends with the human subject, in this case—me. I shall examine Microsoft Windows, Word, and MSN from my point of view as I use them to perform tasks. I hope to show the reader the events and situations I encounter as I use these software applications.

I am concerned with what these software products "present" to me, the user, with what appears to the user, from the user's point of view when using them. I am not concerned with the underlying technical aspects of these software products, that is, with the underlying technology and what goes on behind the scenes. Many people who are far more capable than I am have already written numerous accounts of the Microsoft Windows and related technology. Similarly, I not concerned with a comparison between these Microsoft software products and other, equivalent products on the market. Nor am I interested in a feature-by-feature evaluation of these Microsoft products.

A phenomenological investigation and critique of any subject matter is one that begins and ends with the user's perspective, with what the user encounters while using a product, with what the user finds along the way. I am not concerned with the question of whether or not there is a real, physical dragon under Microsoft's bed; I am concerned with what there is about Microsoft that leads me to see a dragon under that bed.

Similarly, I am not interested in knowing that underlying the phenomenology of colors are chemical reactions or wave length differentiations; I am concerned with the experience of colors, with what I see and how pleasing they are. I am not disputing the fact that what I am calling the technical aspects of a phenomenon may "control" or determine an experience. For example, we know that the neurotransmitter Serotonin binds to receptors and produces electrical signals and emotions; the "experience" of emotions and the thoughts that may occur as the result of electrical signals, however, does not refer to chemicals or electrical signals. Thus, I am not concerned here with what Microsoft would regard as the features of its products. I am concerned, rather, with what they contribute to or detract from work that I use them to do.

Furthermore, I am not concerned with the Windows development technology, or with any of the clever coding underlying these products. I am solely concerned with what these products present to me as tools that I can use to do various things. I am aware of the fact that different technologies allow the production of different results, and that applications produced at any one time depend on the technology available to the developers. However, I do not think that we can blame buggy or badly designed products solely on the technology used. The end result of the examination should be evidence that Windows, Word, and MSN are not user friendly, are not human-centered, and should be junked and re-engineered from scratch.

Who is this Book For?

This book was written primarily for Bill Gates, Chief Software Architect of the Microsoft Corporation, and for anyone who develops Windows or Windows-based software.

I would like to be something like what Socrates was to the Athenians—a gadfly who irritates—and perhaps a goad to get him to make Windows and related software better, much, much better than it is now. I realize, of course, that millions of people have probably communicated their frustrations to Microsoft and that one more will probably have no impact at all. Nevertheless, the Microsoft corporate vision is to "empower" people by producing great software,[3] and listening and responding to users, as Microsoft acknowledges, produce great software.

The book was also written for anyone who has ever used Microsoft Windows, Word, or MSN for work or enjoyment. While some of my experiences with these software applications may be unique, I am sure that many people will have had similar experiences—and will have felt the frustration and have been as infuriated as I have been when using them.

How this Book is Organized

Since the focus of the book is on the user interface, the first chapter is an introduction to the types of user interfaces that we have had to deal with throughout the short life of the personal computer.

---

3 See www.microsoft.com/mscorp.

The second chapter describes the aims involved in the development of Windows and its graphical user interface, then presents a set of criteria to be used to evaluate Windows and related software applications.

Chapters Three, Four, and Five then provide a first-person account of using Windows, Word, and MSN, respectively. The final chapter evaluates these three software applications in light of the criteria presented in Chapter Two.

Conventions

The following more-or-less standard conventions are used throughout the text.

- CAPITALS denote keys and key sequences, as in ALT, and DOS commands.
- Command line examples are indicated by monospaced text.
- The | indicates a path or sequence of selections from a menu, for example FILE|OPEN means open the File menu and select the Open command.
- The + indicates a combination of keys, for example ALT+X means press the ALT and X keys together.

Trademarks

The following terms, used in this book, are trademarks, registered trademarks, or service marks of Microsoft Corporation in the United States and other countries:

Encarta
Hotmail
Internet Explorer
Microsoft
Microsoft Network
Microsoft Word
Microsoft Windows
MS-DOS
MSN
MSN Explorer
Passport
Windows
Word

Other company names or products mentioned in this book may be trademarks, registered trademarks or service marks of their respective owners.

Acknowledgements

I would like to thank the following individuals from IBM who reviewed some of the material contained in this book or provided invaluable feedback and knowledge about the use of Microsoft products in the flow of work: Jeannie Birndorf, Craig Brossman, Brian Doyle, Joe Frick, Brian Haan, Brian Kelly, Ray Knudson, Gary Koets, Scott Mastie, Kendra McConnell, Jim Minor, Bob Niemitalo, Bert Prospero, Judy Reynolds and Tony Stuart. I'd also like to thank Ted Nelson (effective inventor of hypertext and the World Wide Web) for his unremitting (and unrequited) dedication to providing the world with really usable software for home computers and Michael Dertouzos up until his recent death Director of the Laboratory for Computer Science at MIT for his work on behalf of user-centered computing.

Chapter 1

Introduction to PC User Interfaces

The focus of this book is on the way one human being interfaces with three software applications developed by Microsoft. Given this focus, we need to understand the concept of the user interface as well as the evolution of the human-to-machine interface in general and as it applies to personal computers. This chapter thus introduces the concept of the user interface and the various forms it has taken since the introduction of the first personal computer, a little over twenty-five years ago.

What is the Human/Computer Interface?

For much of this century, engineers and psychologists—and what we today call cognitive scientists—have been studying the way human beings interact with machines. Their aim has been to determine the way to design and construct "interfaces" between human users and technological artifacts so that we humans can make the most productive use of them (and, of course, so their makers may get the best return on their investments).

1

Computers consist primarily of a central processing unit (CPU) that is designed to accept inputs (commands to perform some action) from external agents, including humans, to process the command, and then to issue some output or result to the command. The study of how humans of various degrees of expertise, ranging from expert to novice, can most effectively interact or interface with computers to input data or commands and receive output and feedback is a major industry in the academic and business communities.

Understanding, designing, engineering, implementing and using the human to computer interface takes up a great deal of time and effort in the research institutions, such as universities, as well as among businesses that produce computing machines and software. At universities teams of interdisciplinary personnel drawn from fields like management science, psychology, cognitive science, and information technology are on a constant and persistent search for effective ways of managing the "dialogs" that human engage in with computers. In companies that develop computer software, there are usually people, generally called human factors experts, performing similar tasks. The study and development of the user interface has this "dialog" between human and computer as its primary focus. What sorts of inputs can humans make to the computer, and what sorts of outputs may be expected?

In the evolution of the personal computer, we can identify four distinct metaphors that have been used to characterize the form or model of this user interface. This introduction will describe these metaphors and the type of user interface that they involve.

Switches and Flashing Lights

Though dreamt, written and talked about for years before this, the personal computer boom began when a small Albuquerque, New Mexico, company called MITS advertised its Altair 8800 computer in *Popular Electronics* in January 1975. In kit form, the Altair cost $395; assembled, it was $495. By April, 4000 people had ordered one. The Altair featured a BASIC programming language written by Bill Gates and Paul Allen, founders of Microsoft, whose first customer was MITS.

The Altair was a box-shaped machine that measured 17x18x7 inches. It had no keyboard or paper tape reader for input, and no output devices like a video terminal or printer. The user interface consisted of toggle switches used to make inputs to the computer and flashing lights on the front panel for outputs.

To enter program commands or data, you had to set the toggle switches on the front, for all programming was in the machine code of binary digits. The results of a program (or command) were indicated by the pattern of flashing lights on the front panel.

This early personal computer was for hobbyists and experts in talking in machine language to computers, and even though we may cringe at such a primitive user interface, switches and flashing lights remain a major part of current user interfaces. For example, Windows has numerous buttons that a user can affirm with a checkmark or deny with a blank, and the famous hourglass that indicates a load (or start) process that is still pending is similar to a flashing light.

The Command Line

The Altair was soon followed by a slew of computers from different companies such as Apple, Processor Technology (Sol), Osborne and others that featured an improved user interface. Now, there was at least a keyboard for input and an electronic monitor (CRT) for output.

It was, however, the hugely successful Apple II from Apple Computers in 1977 that really opened the door. But in spite of the success of the Apple II and subsequent lines of Apple computers, it wasn't until a few brash young men bamboozled IBM with an operating system called MS-DOS that IBM installed into its IBM PC in 1981 that the personal computing revolution really took off.

On all of the computers that followed the Altair, users were provided with a command line (on the video terminal) where "commands" (to do something) could be communicated (entered into) the computer from the keyboard and the computer would respond. From their inception, their creators endowed these personal computers with an "interpreter" (indicated by a prompt of some kind) that accepted keyboard-entered commands from users, interpreted their validity and, if valid, executed them and "returned" the result to the user on a screen.

So, for example, a user could enter a command like:

```
C:\>Print "Hello World"
```

And the computer would respond with:

```
Hello World
```

The MS-DOS Operating System

The commands that could be entered to the prompt on the IBM PC and its clones, universally known as the "C prompt" (modifications and disk partitions resulting in "D", "E" and other prompts came later), were all stored in the COMMAND.COM file and contained the infamous MS-DOS operating system.

The commands were defined and explained, and occasionally illustrated, in DOS reference manuals that listed the commands most often in alphabetical order. Little has changed since then, except that the command interpreter later came to be called CMD.EXE on some machines. But whatever the name, COMMAND.COM is still found in the root directory of all IBM PC type machines.

Learning MS-DOS Commands

Users learnt commands by trying each one listed in the DOS manuals that came with their computers:

- If you wanted to copy one file to another name, you used the COPY command

- If you wanted to copy an entire diskette to another diskette, you used the DCOPY command

- If you wanted to join the end of one file to start of another, you used the APPEND command

- If you wanted to see the contents of a text file, you used the TYPE command

Batch Files

Included with MS-DOS was a simplified "batch" processing language (whose files ended with the extension "bat") that could be used to create "programs" to run a set of the DOS commands as a batch, and the "*program*.bat" program was itself considered a "command" that could be executed (or run) when desired.

Expert users would learn the whole set of commands associated with the machines; the DOS command reference with its complex and involved command syntax (and relatively few examples or cautions) was a constant on all desks.

Novice users contented themselves with learning to use a few of the simpler commands, like SAVE, COPY, TYPE and RUN. Bridging the gap between the majority of users who were novices and the few who were experts were the technical support personnel, one of the major growth industries of the personal computer revolution.

Problems with the Command Line Interface

One of the major problems with the command line interface is hinted at above. To use DOS effectively, one had to learn a complex syntax. Remembering all of the options and parameters of each command, not to mention remembering all of the different commands, placed an undue burden on the cognitive abilities of most users. Since most experts (like programmers and hackers) couldn't be bothered with the host of novice users, technical support evolved as an intermediary between the two.

Another, related problem is that some of the DOS commands had to be preformed in a certain order, yet the commands themselves carried nothing in their structure indicating that there were commands that had to be performed either before or after them. Thus if one wanted to COPY a file to a diskette, one had to remember to FORMAT the diskette first.

A related problem is that though there was some help associated with each command, this took the form mainly of syntax diagrams. There were no warning messages and there were no messages that could help to understand a problem that occurred when using a command.

Similarly, some commands had unexpected (and unwanted) consequences, yet couldn't be reversed. If you erased a file from DOS, that was it. If you did a Format C instead of a FORMAT A, you wiped out your hard disk. Commands like ASSIGN and others had similar liabilities.

Like the switches and flashing light interface of the Altair, the command line remains a part of the user interface in more recent interfaces. On the Internet, for example, when one enters a URL (like http://www.blah.blah), one is entering a command on a command line. When one accesses MS-DOS either through a Windows window or by directly loading it so as to resolve a dead Windows problem, one is using the command line. And, in fact, opening a program from the Windows desktop is very similar to executing a command from the command line—except that the command and its syntax is pre-programmed and instead of just pressing Return or Enter to run the command, one clicks an icon.

Menus

One of the ways in which some of these problems were resolved was by the use of lists of commands called menus. As the list of commands grew larger and larger and particularly as the list of procedure-based programs grew, so did the list of users, more and more of whom had no desire to become experts in command set usage, but simply wanted to do their jobs and go home.

Lists of Commands

The proliferation of non-expert users led to the development of menus of commands. Where applications once gave users an alphabetical list of commands and sometimes instructions on when and where to run the commands, the move was made to an ordered list of commands in menus and submenus. Who among us does not remember the days when you were toast if you ran the General Ledger before running and booking all accounts, or when 10MB of data (that is, everything on your hard disk) were lost because someone wanted to experiment with the FORMAT command (or typed FORMAT C instead of FORMAT A, in the days when you had to format your own diskettes)?

Introducing order to the Command List

Menus introduced some order into the set of commands. The order could be ordinal only, so that the user would know the set of commands available at any point (these were generally issued under program control) and could select 1, 2, or 3, press Return or Enter and go to the appropriate screen. Alternatively, some menus provided a set of items in a cardinal order (first, second, third...) and users were expected to perform the commands in the order specified.

Such a use of menus helped to resolve the problem of remembering complex command syntax and rules. Users no longer had to memorize or remember commands and their syntax. Menus also helped to give some order to the atomistic list of operating system (or application) commands. Since help messages could be associated with menu items, more help was provided to the ordinary, novice user.

Of course, there is a vast literature associated with the study of menus as a form of the user interface. There are many types of menus (such as single, sequential linear, hierarchical, or event trap), and there are many complex reasons for using or not using menus as specific points in an application. These studies are ongoing. They involve teams of cognitive scientists and related disciplines.

Menus are a key ingredient of the graphical user interface (GUI) that superseded the command line and the menu interfaces. Windows itself and all applications based on Windows feature a usually vast array of pull-down and other types of menus. The effectiveness of these menus is something we will be considering as we examine those three key Microsoft applications, Windows, Word and MSN.

The Graphical User Interface

The Graphical User Interface (GUI), the next step in the evolution of the user interface, was invented by Xerox at its Palo Alto Research Center (PARC) in the 1970's and was implemented on a couple of Xerox computers, but it wasn't until 1983 when Apple used a GUI interface on its LISA computer that a commercially viable product with a GUI was introduced to the market. In 1985, Microsoft introduced its Windows 1.0 that implemented a GUI on the IBM PC.

The rest, as they say, is history.

While Apple GUIs enjoyed a relative degree of success in the 1980's, when Microsoft introduced its Windows 3.1 in 1992, the GUI-based world really took off. Though Apple continues to produce GUI products on its proprietary OS, and even though Unix has a windows look alike GUI called X Windows, over ninety percent of the personal computing world uses the Microsoft GUI as implemented in its Windows products.

The GUI is supposed to provide us with an intuitive (i.e., understandable), easy-to-use way of running and using applications, including the "application" of setting up and configuring the computer. It is supposed to shield users from the intricacies and the arcane syntax of the command line (though, thankfully, Microsoft, unlike Apple, gives us easy access to the command line, where things like making directories or folders are far easier done than through the GUI). The GUI is supposed to provide us with "productivity enhancing" tools. It is supposed to make our jobs easier and more fun. It is supposed to help us soar!

But does it? At least as implemented on Microsoft Windows and related products, is the GUI all it's proclaimed to be?

What's Wrong with the GUI

In this book, I am going to take an admittedly skeptical view of these sorts of claims. I want to look at Microsoft Windows (a so-called operating system), Microsoft Word (a widely used application for Windows) and the Microsoft Network (MSN) all with the aim of evaluating the claims made in support of the GUI and how it is supposed to make us all more productive.

While it may be true that a GUI is inherently capable of doing the things claimed for it, I shall attempt to show that in the case of the three items noted above, it fails. I rather suspect that any GUI environment or OS (from Apple, Unix, or anyone else), if subjected to the same analysis, would also result in the same conclusion. GUIs may eventually provide heaven on earth for computer users, but not as currently implemented.

Chapter 2

Criteria for Evaluating Microsoft Software

In this book, our attention is directed on the graphical user interface (GUI) model of the user interface as it is implemented in Microsoft Windows, Word for Windows, and the Microsoft Network applications. Since the Windows GUI is the foundation for all three applications, we need to understand what Microsoft Windows is designed to do. We also need this information because it will provide the set of standards or the criteria against which the three applications can be evaluated.

The GUI Timeline

To better understand the Microsoft Windows GUI, we need some orientation to the historical context in which Microsoft Windows was developed.

The first known GUI was implemented on the Alto computer in April 1973 at the Xerox PARC. It featured a three-button mouse, a bit-mapped display, and graphic windows. Eight years later, in

June 1981, the Xerox Star computer introduced icons that could be double-clicked, overlapping windows, and dialog boxes. These two computers were never sold or marketed by Xerox, however.

In January of 1983, a few years after the highly successful Apple II with its command line and menu interfaces Apple introduced the LISA computer with pull-down menus and menu bars. This computer did not enjoy economic success.

In August 1985, Microsoft introduced Windows 1.0 with tiled, but not overlapping windows, and an area at the bottom of the screen reserved for icons. In 1987, Windows 2.03 introduced resizable windows then in May 1990, Windows 3.0 was introduced. This is when the Windows phenomenon began to proliferate rapidly. By the time Windows 3.1 was introduced in March 1992, Windows now included multi-media capabilities.

Since the introduction of Windows 3.1, the growth of Microsoft and the use of Windows on IBM type PCs have been phenomenal. This version of Windows was followed by two different flavors of Windows. One flavor was intended for the use of individuals and small businesses and included Windows 95, Windows 98, Windows 2000 and Windows ME, all of which involved enhancements or extensions of the MS-DOS operating system. The other flavor of Windows was the NT, which was intended for the use of businesses and was based on a different "kernel" than MS-DOS. Now, Windows XP brings these two flavors of Windows back together, with one kernel used for all Windows flavors.

Microsoft's View of the Windows GUI

Though building on the work of other GUI developers, Microsoft Windows represents a specific flavor of the GUI. We need to understand what Microsoft intended to provide with its Windows GUI if we are to be in a position to evaluate its implementations in Windows itself, and in Word and MSN.

Windows

In its article on "Windows" in Microsoft Encarta Online Encyclopedia 2001[4], Microsoft defines Windows as a "personal computer operating system" that is an extension of and replacement for MS-DOS. It incorporates a GUI that allows users to manipulate icons on the screen to run commands.

Windows are frames created on the desktop screen in which commands are run. Strictly speaking, of course, the menu user interface, which existed long before icons, was a way of running commands by selecting verbal instead of iconic representations of them. Many Windows applications also use menus of commands that have no iconic representation.

GUI

In the same place, Microsoft further describes the GUI as a "natural or intuitive" work environment for the user. This is explained as an environment where the user can move a cursor around on the screen with a point-and-click device like a mouse to perform actions that are stored as commands and are accessible either

---

4 See encarta.msn.com.

directly on the screen or indirectly through menus. This type of GUI is described as having WIMP features, for it includes windows, icons, menus, and a pointing device.

Features of Windows

A "natural or intuitive" Windows GUI thus provides the following features.

- First, the user is provided with applications that are run in windows.

- Second, commands are executed by pointing to icons instead of typing.

- Third, commands are grouped together into (presumably logical) menus.

- Fourth, commands are entered with a "mouse" (or other pointing device) instead of a keyboard, permitting the use of one hand instead of two, for the most part.

In the same Encarta article mentioned above, Microsoft informs us that Windows 95 provides a "sleeker and simpler" GUI than previous Windows releases, and that subsequent Windows releases improve on their predecessors. From this we can gather that Microsoft thinks that Windows 98 is sleeker and simpler than Windows 95, and so on.

Natural or Intuitive Work Environment

Now, the four features of the GUI are important to the definition of a Windows environment, but tell us nothing more than we would know were a car salesman to tell us that he sells machines with wheels and a steering mechanism.

What is more of interest is the "intention" of creating a Windows environment—it is to provide the user with a "natural" or "intuitive" working environment. Of course, just exactly what the designers and developers of Windows technology had/have in mind when they talk about a natural or intuitive work environment is subject to interpretation and controversy. However, we should be able to eke out at least some general expectations about what this intention entails.

What is a Natural Work Environment?

What is a natural or intuitive work environment? What makes a work environment natural or intuitive?

Microsoft obviously thinks that its Windows product provides a natural or intuitive work environment, or at least makes a good attempt to do so. But just what the criteria for success are in this matter is not at all clear.

Of course, as Microsoft would be the first to admit, determining exactly how to design software that is natural or intuitive is difficult to determine. The Microsoft developer's network (msdn.microsoft.com) is replete with articles describing their design efforts and their involvement of writers, developers, and human factors personnel in the whole development process.

User Types

When we speak of an "intuitive" piece of software, we at a minimum mean one where the user, of whichever type (technical or ordinary), is able to understand and adapt to the software with relative ease—and to be productive using it within a reasonable amount of time. An "unintuitive" software product, on the other hand, would be hard to understand, hard to use, and difficult to use productively within a reasonable period of time.

So, the first thing we have to do is distinguish between different types of users. One set of users of a Windows environment is technical people very much like the technical types who design and develop the environment. Another set of users is the vastly larger set of people who have no knowledge of or interest in the technical features of some piece of software, but simply have a job to be done. The first set, the technical users may be said to use (or develop) software as an **end** in self; the more ordinary users use software as a **means** to an end. So, for which of these two types of users is Windows a natural work environment? Or, is the environment supposed to be natural for both groups?

Flow of Work

Another feature of a natural or intuitive work environment follows from this understanding of people. Since people work by performing tasks, and tasks on a computer are initiated through commands, a natural or intuitive work environment is one which is organized logically so that users (workers) can find the commands they need for their work by tracing easy to follow paths.

This means that we should expect a coherent environment that is consistent and predictable. A user (worker) must be able to use the application and perform work with it. Microsoft and other Windows and Windows-related application developers are constantly telling us how productive we can be using their software. Maybe so, but the question remains: are we really more productive using Windows, Word, and MSN or are we wasting a lot of time on tasks that are badly designed?

Still another feature of a natural or intuitive work environment is that the user has access to help when about to perform a task as well as while performing a task. This means, essentially, that help information is provided on tasks (commands) before and while performing them in the form of a help system that can be accessed before performing a task to learn how to do it, and while performing the task in the form of feedback and contextual help.

Criteria for Evaluation

The WIMP (windows, icons, menus, and pointing device) features that characterize the Microsoft Windows GUI are supposed to provide us with a natural or intuitive work environment. In addition to evaluating the use of the WIMP factors, we also need to evaluate how well the three Microsoft products perform as contributors to the flow of work.

I have reduced the features of what I believe a natural or intuitive work environment means to four simple rules:

- Minimize contact with the internals of the software for non-expert users

- Minimize the need for technical knowledge for non-expert users

- Minimize the need to search far and wide for commands by optimizing the use of logical menus

- Optimize the availability of help information

While I cannot assert that these features were intentionally included within the Microsoft suite of Windows software, I think it is reasonable to expect that natural or intuitive software should include them. At any rate, I will use these expected features as the standards to evaluate whether or not this user thinks that Microsoft has successfully implemented a natural or intuitive GUI in any one or all three of the applications we will be using and considering in this book.

Chapter 3

Microsoft Windows

This chapter describes one user's encounter with the "natural or intuitive" work environment provided by the WIMP factors in Microsoft Windows. The focus of this chapter is Windows 98, Version 4.10.222, though I indicate changes and improvements that have been made by Windows XP, which is just arriving on the market. My view is that the later versions of Windows, including Windows XP, still suffer from the same problems that I report on here about Windows 98.

MS-DOS

As we noted in the previous chapter, Microsoft regards Windows as a replacement for and enhancement of MS-DOS. The user interface provided by Windows is one that uses, among other things, iconic representations of DOS (and other) commands that allow users to run commands without having to learn or remember the often complex and arcane syntax of those commands.

As we begin this journey through the Windows environment, it may be worth our while to recall just what it is that the Windows user interface replaced.

MS-DOS Commands

Microsoft DOS version 1.0 was the operating system included on the IBM PC in 1981, the first IBM type PC. The user interface of this machine was the command line supplemented by menus. The final version of MS-DOS was created in 1994 as version 6.22. The commands in this set are listed below:

ANSI.SYS | APPEND | ARP | ASSIGN | ATTRIB
BREAK
CD | CHCP | CHDIR | CHKDSK | CHOICE | CLS | COMMAND
   | COPY | CTTY
DATE | DEBUG | DEFRAG | DEL | DELTREE | DIR |
DISKCOMP | DISKCOPY | DOSKEY | DOSSHELL | DRIVPARM
ECHO | EDIT | EDLIN | EMM386 | ERASE | EXIT | EXPAND
   | EXTRACT
FASTHELP | FC | FDISK | FIND | FOR | FORMAT | FTP
HELP
IFSHLP.SYS | IPCONFIG
KEYB
LABEL | LH | LOADFIX | LOADHIGH | LOCK
MD | MEM | MKDIR | MODE | MORE | MOVE | MSAV |
   MSD | MSCDEX
NET | NLSFUNC
PATH | PAUSE | PING | POWER | PRINT | PROMPT
QBASIC
RD | REN | RENAME | RMDIR | ROUTE

SCANDISK | SCANREG | SET | SETVER | SHARE | SORT |
   SUBST |
SWITCHES | SYS
TIME | TRACERT | TREE | TYPE
UNDELETE | UNFORMAT | UNLOCK
VER | VERIFY | VOL
XCOPY

In addition to these commands, there are others that are either proprietary or secret and were not documented in the DOS Command references of the day.

Running DOS Commands

To run an MS-DOS command, you would type it in at the C:> prompt and press Return or Enter. Commands like QBASIC opened a new environment in which new commands could be created. BAT files, using a primitive scripting system, could also be written to create new commands. Similarly, applications were accessed via commands.

If you were an ordinary user, you soon learnt to use straightforward commands like CD (change directory), CLS (clear screen), COPY, EDIT (for the word processor), EDLIN (for a really primitive word processor), FORMAT (so you could backup your work on a diskette or floppy), HELP (to display the syntax for DOS commands), MD (to create directories, nowadays called folders), MORE, PRINT, RD (to remove directories), and TYPE. Programmers and other technical types would use these as well as other more complex commands.

Most of the commands had a variety of arguments and options. For example, to use COPY, you had to be able to specify the thing to be copied and the place to which it was to be copied. Other commands had numerous options, and anyone who issued them had to be constantly referencing a command manual (or the help facility)—and eventually many of us just memorized as much as we could.

It was around this time that the major growth industry of the PC era mushroomed, namely technical support. Expert users of DOS commands were too busy or lacked interest in helping novice or non-technical users with DOS commands, so there arose this industry to mediate the technical and the non-technical user.

DOS and Windows

The DOS command line environment of the early PC is what Windows claims to replace. We need to note, however, that MS-DOS is an operating system. Microsoft might like to claim that Windows is an operating system itself, but Windows still uses DOS; Windows sits on top of DOS, and to this day, DOS commands can be issued by accessing a DOS window and typing commands in at the DOS prompt. Many commands that can be issued in the Windows environment (such as from Windows Explorer) can more easily be done "in" DOS.

In addition to accessing DOS from a Windows window, Windows can be bypassed entirely by booting up the machine in MS-DOS. Microsoft may claim that Windows is an operating system, but when Windows crashes, which it often does in Windows 95, 98 and others, the only recourse is to bypass Windows by going directly into DOS to repair the machine. From DOS, the WIN command could be used to bring Windows up.

Similarly there are software companies that have developed software that bypasses Windows entirely by relying either on

DOS alone or loading another operating system, such as Linux, on top of DOS. But no matter the case, and no matter how much Microsoft claims that Windows is an OS, it isn't—it is at best a parasite of DOS. Now that XP is supposed to usher in a new kernel for Windows that bypasses DOS, we shall see what happens when and if Windows crashes.

Booting up

Let us begin our examination of the Windows replacement for DOS by starting at the beginning—booting the machine. Here I want to compare the boot process on the old IBM XT machines of the early 1980's to the twenty-first century boot process of Windows 98.

Booting up an XT with DOS

I turn on my good old IBM XT computer with 10 MB of disk, and what is it, 16K of RAM and a less than 1 MHZ CPU, and as soon as the phosphor warms up (less than 30 seconds), the DOS prompt is blinking at me and work can begin for the day. It's "natural" to me that I turn something "on" and it's ready to go. Even on cold days, the car starts right away and takes only a little while to warm up. It's natural that technology, mechanical or electronic, is "available" to me when I want it.

Booting up in Windows 98

So, let's try Windows. I have Windows 98 running only a 500MHZ machine with 4 Gigs of disk and 128 MB of RAM. In effect, my current machine has a CPU that is allegedly 500 times faster than the old XT, has 400 times the disk space, and about 8,000 times more memory.

Turn the machine on...and WAIT! Time for a cup or two of coffee, a few cigarettes, do the laundry...while Windows 98 loads:

- First, Compaq informs me that this is a Compaq machine, when right below the screen it tells me the same thing.

- Then there's a bit of cracking and the Windows 98 screen flicks on momentarily.

- Then we go into DOS and I see a bunch of DOS commands (usually the path and a few messages, like "Please wait, Windows is loading," as if I wouldn't have been able to guess).

- Then the Windows 98 screen appears again momentarily.

- Then it's back into DOS (showing pretty much what the previous DOS screen showed).

- Then, finally, the main screen, called the "desktop" begins to appear.

Whew! So now, instead of thirty seconds and on to work, we have a considerably faster CPU, a great deal more disk space, about 8000 times more RAM, yet it still takes several minutes before I can get to work. This is an improvement?

Let's see, 100 million Windows being opened every day in the USA alone; let's say it takes 3 minutes—of lost productivity. That comes out to 5 million hours a day, one billion a year. What's the normal charge? Make that $20.00 per hour (this is the $120 per of technical workers averaged out to include the "less skilled"). Industry can invoice Bill Gates for $20 billion a year in lost productivity—and this is just for booting Windows, without trying to DO anything with it, yet!

Booting up Windows XP

Windows XP, due for release in late 2001, is a new version of Windows with a new kernel that is supposed to be better in speed and performance (not to mention stability and user friendliness). To use this version of Windows, the minimum requirements are a 300Mhz machine with at least 128 MB of memory.

These requirements should make one suspicious. XP adds considerably more functionality to Windows, for one thing. These minimum requirements also suggest that we have an even more memory-intensive and CPU hog than we had before. But we can leave this question open for now, since it will take some time and experience before the boot process for XP can be evaluated. One generally needs a few months of using a Windows release before such an evaluation can take place.

The Desktop

The "desktop" is the metaphor that Microsoft uses to refer to the main screen that comes up when Windows is loaded. On Windows 98, the desktop displays numerous icons as a default. Windows XP, on the other hand, has fewer displayed icons than previous Windows releases, so some of the comments about icons on the desktop may not apply to the XP release.

The Desktop Metaphor

Now I don't know about you, but I use my desk to work on, and my bookcases and side tables for storing the things I may work on. When I look at the Windows "desktop" I don't see a desktop—I see a bunch of storage bins, bookshelves, a warehouse or whatever else you want to call them—but don't call it a desktop.

The metaphor is hardly appropriate—and it is entirely misleading. A more appropriate metaphor might be the tool shed or the warehouse or the bookcase or the file cabinet...But "desktop"? Who, on earth, came up with this howler? It is not natural or intuitive. The metaphor is not a "real world" metaphor.

I understand the reasons for calling the principal window that is displayed when Windows is loaded a desktop, but it really is a picture window or a grand overview of all of the applications that are available to me when I load the Windows environment.

Desktop Icons

Well, let's look at this desktop. Mine shows around 30 items using large icons, which take up most of the screen. With small icons, half the screen is taken up. On XP, the desktop appears less cluttered with icons, but that may or may not be an improvement. The items on the desktop are applications that are represented by an icon and a text title.

What is the good of the icons—other than taking up unnecessary space? Take a look at the icons on your desktop. Most of them have no resemblance to what they describe. Many are company logos. What is the point of including icons on the "desktop"? Is this supposed to be a way of familiarizing new users with the idea that you click icons to launch applications? Surely, after the first couple of times, at most, this function ceases to have any value.

If I were able to get rid of the icons on the desktop and use only text descriptions, I could at least triple the number of items I could show on my desktop. There's no way of getting rid of these icons, however—except possibly through a circuitous hack.[5] So, I'm forced (unnaturally, I might add) to accept useless items (icons) on my desktop (which is really a tool shed or warehouse). I could eliminate the text by renaming the icon with an empty string, but then I wouldn't be able to recognize most of the items on the desktop (with due apologies to those who've labored mightily to produce intelligible logos for their companies). I'd be lost without the text, but the icons I could do without.[6]

Arranging the Desktop

Windows provides a popup dialog to enable a user to personalize the desktop (right click on a blank area of the desktop). You can add new shortcuts, delete those you don't want, arrange the items in various ways, and customize the appearance of the desktop.

Let's try customizing the appearance of the desktop. From the menu that appears, click "Properties." A tabbed dialog appears that allows one to customize background pictures, screen saver,

---

5   Since the icons are bitmaps, one could create a tiny and empty bitmap then replace all existing icons with it, but this would be a hassle. XP reduces the number of icons on the desktop but does not eliminate their use.

6   The only icon I recognize immediately is the MS-DOS icon, but that icon includes the text MS-DOS.

visual effects, effects when the desktop works like a web page, and settings.

Desktop Properties

The first thing to note is that the "Settings" tab is the last in the list, yet it is through this tab that one can specify the type of monitor being used to display the desktop; logically, this tab should be the first in the list of tabs. Through it, one can also specify the number of colors that are to be used on the display. One reason why this tab is placed here, however, is that in addition to these settings, one can also make "advanced" adjustments to the display.

However, given that just about every "adjustment" one can make to the default settings on Windows involves something of a hack (this means that you need to evaluate the tweak by asking those who know better, write down your changes, back up the entire system if you have such a capability, and say a prayer that everything doesn't go haywire from your supposedly innocuous tweak), it's just as well that these "advanced" adjustments to the display are listed last.

No Help for Desktop Icons

It's nice that one can customize the picture on the background and on the screen saver. It's also nice that there is a context help feature associated with the dialog, though when I clicked on "Desktop Icons" under "Effects" all I got was that infamous dialog:

```
No help topic is associated with this item
```

Web Tab Dialogs

A similar disconcerting event takes place when you go to the "Web" tab. Near to the bottom, the tab informs you:

```
To change the way you click a desktop item, click:
Folder Options
```

When clicked, a dialog displays that asks:

```
Would you like to save and close the display
properties and view the folder options instead?
Yes No
```

This is a bad piece of design in an otherwise nice function. The transition into folder options could have been better made. I have no idea what the dialog is asking me to do, nor do I know the consequences of saying "yes." Also, the dialog is superfluous: why else would I have clicked the Folder Options? Why have a dialog like this one here when such a transition isn't used in other places? I attribute this messy transition to laziness.

Arrange Alphabetically

Let's turn now to some functions that are provided to arrange the (what I think are useless and pointless) icons on the desktop.

The first tool for arranging the icons is by name, with the standard default in ascending order, from A to Z. When I select this function, the following effects occur:

- "My Computer" is still in the upper left-hand corner where the A's should be.

- Immediately below, in the same column are: My Documents, IE, Recycle, and Briefcase. (This arrangement is hardly an alphabetical one but I suppose the reasoning is that these "standard" desktop items should always be listed in the leftmost column, but note that they're not placed into alphabetical order.)

- "Microsoft Word" and MSN Explorer are under M, rather than W and N or E. Outlook Express, on the other hand, though also a Microsoft product is placed under O.

- Windows Explorer, a Windows function that essentially replaces the DOS DIR command, is under W, while it would make much more sense under E.

Essentially, then, the alphabetization function is useless.

Arrange by Type

Let's now try arranging the icons by type. As before, the standard icons are in the left column. Then the system arranges:

Real.com Guide
Acrobat Reader
Calc
CD Player
Word
MPlayer
Paint
Notepad
Outlook Express
Ping
ISP
Real Download

Jukebox
WordPad
MS-DOS

Well, intuitively one would have expected to find the word processors (Word, WordPad, Notepad) grouped together; and MPlayer, Jukebox, Player, and CD Player grouped together. But they aren't. This is another useless function.

Arrange by Size

Let's now try arranging icons by size. Now, while arrangement by size makes little sense as a way of arranging the desktop, it does supply some useful information. Not surprisingly, we find that Microsoft Word is the largest application on the desktop. So, we can let this function pass—as an information provider rather than as a way of arranging things.

Arrange by Date

Like arrange by size, arrange by date is an information provider. Since the desktop is not exactly an inventory control system, a date arrangement only gives me some insight into the temporal order in which I installed the application icons.

Other Types of Arrangement

I look in vain for other types of desktop arrangement tools. It is somewhat odd that Microsoft supplies all of these "customization" options with Windows, yet the option of arranging the desktop itself is nowhere to be found. Here are some of the things I'd like to do to arrange my desktop.

Split the Desktop into Two

I'd like to be able to split the desktop screen into two vertically or horizontally split windows: one to show my icons (tools) and one to run my applications.

This would be like the "tree" view of data such as we have in Windows or the Windows Help system, which shows the list of topics on the left and displays the content of a topic on the right side. As it stands now, launching an application either replaces the window, or runs in another restored or maximized window. I'd like to be able to keep the desktop items always visible (on top) **and** the launched application visible at the same time.

The Quick Launch toolbar is a step in this direction, but it's not exactly what I want. I can, of course, access the desktop from the QL toolbar, but that means going back and forth, while what I want is to move the cursor (or mouse pointer) from a top (or bottom) window which is running an application to the bottom (or top) window where the available applications are always displayed.

Move the Start Menu

I'd also like to be able to move the Start menu to some other corner of the desktop screen. But no, you have to take what Microsoft gives you. Of course, I suppose one could always go poking around in the code and do some hacking to get stuff like this done, but who among us—omitting developers and born hackers—has the time or courage to risk wrecking the system just for a little personalization?

We should also note that while the Properties option has a tabbed dialog with context-specific help, none of the other functions have help associated with them. To get help one has to access the Windows Help system, which is quite extensive in its range of topics, but also relatively useless as a place to find what one is looking for. A little consistency on the designer's part (or was this designed by the Chief Software Architect himself?) would have been nice.

The Start Menu

One of the features of the Windows environment is that in addition to providing users with a "desktop" of applications (represented by icons) in a windows framework it also retains and provides the menu-based method of running these applications. The "Start" menu system provides users with menus (lists) of all (or most) installed programs and utilities, including Windows system programs, user-installed applications, and also the method of running programs stored on external media. This is a worthwhile feature.

Contents of the Start Menu

Upon accessing the Start menu, users can access the above-mentioned programs, the web pages stored under their "Favorites," Documents, System Settings (also accessible from the Control Panel, discussed later) . They can also use the Find and Help utilities, Log off a user (if there are multiple users of the machine), and Shut Down the computer in a variety of ways (including direct access to MS-DOS, if necessary to perform certain functions).

XP has made a few minor changes to this menu, mainly affecting the layout and providing more colorful icons, but nothing substantial. On the left side this XP menu now lists the user's most frequently used programs, while on the right are user directories and system utilities.

Reorganizing the Start menu in Windows XP may be a way of improving the usability of the function, but that effect is not obvious. I suppose that moving the selection to access the list of programs from the top of the menu (Windows 98) to the bottom of the menu (Windows XP) is a usability feature, but whether or not it provides an improvement in the way Windows is used is a moot question at this point.

Lacks Context-specific Help

Lacking from the Start menu is a context-specific help system. The designers of the Windows OS need to work on making the help system context-specific throughout the system, on all panels, all dialogs, and all menus. Since I have developed Windows-based applications where every item has a context-specific help topic, I know that this can be done.

Not only does each layer of the Start menu need context-specific help but the options on some (or all) of these menus need to be defined and explained. The set of System Tools under the Accessories menu, for example, need to be explained. For example, all of the System Tools accessible by the Start | Programs | Accessories path could use some context help. What does Scandisk do? What about DriveSpace or Disk Cleanup? Lacking a context-specific help system, one must first write down the functions one is interested in knowing about then either read the hardcopy manual or else access the help system and investigate each of these items in turn before, finally, returning to the Start menu and proceeding with one's tasks.

Repetitive Path Tracing

One of the most annoying features of the Start menu, to me, is that once one has traced a path from Start to some point in the menu tree and has made a selection, the menu disappears and one has to trace the path all over again for the next item one wants to check out. It would be nice to have had the ability to right click to a "Stay Put" option instead.

For example, let's say that I am a interested in "Viewing" the features of various programs (something that admittedly only a programmer would want to do), then I must trace the following path:

Start I Programs I Accessories I Notepad I Right Button I Quick View

If I then want to run the program in question, I must follow the same path once again, this time selecting Open instead of Quick View. By the third time, this is a real pain in the butt and issues in many aspersions being cast on the origin and destination of the Windows designers and development crew. My list of Favorites, for instance, will preserve the place of my last visit so I do not have to scroll the entire list every time I open it. If this can be done in Favorites, it surely can also be done for the Start menu.

Menu Layers

Microsoft uses an excessive number of menu layers in the Start menu. We have seen one instance in the previous section on repetitive path tracing, but the entire menu is riddled with menu layers that are excessive.

Assume that you want to access the Clipboard Viewer to see what, if anything, you've placed on the Clipboard. Here is the path you must trace:

- Start menu
- Programs
- Accessories
- System Tools
- Clipboard Viewer

Suppose you want to check the free space and other attributes of your disk drives then speed up the opening of files by turning compression (if you use it) off? You would trace this path:

- Start menu
- Programs
- Accessories
- System Tools
- DriveSpace
- Drive menu
- Properties (to check your free, used, and available disk space)
- Exit
- Advanced menu
- Settings

- Click or unclick compression option
- OK
- OK

Ouch! I rest my case.

Right Click Menu

Another nit is the pull-down menu accessed by right clicking on a selected item. This pull-down is not context-specific, but general. For example, what's the point of including a "Sort by Name" option when one has selected a single item, like Notepad?

Also, the Rename function renames the function only for that location (on the Start menu) and does not extend to the application's name on the desktop. So, if I want to rename a program, I can do so only by accessing every location where it might be stored. As the wit noted, the man with two watches never knows the correct time. So, if you have to change something's name in more than one place, you never know if you've changed it everywhere.

Standard Desktop Utilities

All right, we have now covered most of the items on and surrounding the desktop. Now we need to take a look at the standard utilities on the desktop: Windows Explorer, Documents, Recycle Bin, My Briefcase and My Computer.

Windows Explorer

Windows Explorer performs the function of the DOS DIR command without having to do all the directory changes (CDs). Instead of all that typing, you can explore the drives, folders, and files on the hard drives and perform many different functions on them—copying, deleting, renaming, moving, and so on.

File Properties

Of course, as is usually the case with Windows, some things that DOS did automatically require additional mouse strokes under Windows.

For example, the end result of every DOS DIR command is a record of the size of every displayed file, including the date last changed. Under Explorer, on the other hand, one must first select the file, right-click for a pull-down menu then select Properties for a view of the size of the selected file. In addition, however, Explorer displays the last date viewed, modified, and when created, so I suppose the extra mouse clicks under Windows are compensated for by the extra date information. But having to go down three layers in a menu system to get this data seems a bit much.

Excessive Menu Depth

The Windows Explorer exhibits one of the key negative features of Windows—excessive depth of menus. One of the keys to a successfully human-centered menu system is that menu layers in a hierarchical menu system such as we find in Windows should be **shallow** rather than deep. A shallow menu system has at most three layers; a deep one exceeds that number of layers.

In Windows, the layers of the menu system are not only deep, but are excessively deep. It is often necessary to go down five, six, seven or more layers to perform a simple task. Take, for example, the matter of displaying or not displaying file extensions. Sometimes I like to be able to see the extensions of the files in my different folders (or directories); sometimes I don't care to see them. One would think that there would be an option called "File Extensions" on the file menu that would allow a click on or off for this function.

That, however, is not the case. If you want to reveal or conceal file extensions, you must traverse the following path:

- Start at the desktop.
- Access Windows Explorer.
- Select a folder.
- Open the View menu. (Why not the File menu?)
- Select Folder Options.
- Access the View tab and check or uncheck the line that says "Hide file extensions for known file types."
- If you want this action to apply to all folders (not just the folder selected in Step 3), press the button with the title "Like Current Folders" on the Folder View part of the tab.

This is a seven-step process that could have taken at most three steps if this option had been included in the File or View menus as an option. Microsoft loves to complicate things that could be simple. The principle of Parsimony is unknown among the developers.

My Briefcase

My Briefcase replaces the old DOS function of copying files to a diskette, loading them on some other machine to work on them, then "synchronizing" the two sets of files by once again over-writing the files on the original machine drive. With the Browse function, one can avoid many of the directory changes (CD) required if one were to do this from DOS.

Recycle Bin

The Recycle Bin is appropriately named. It is, after all, a tempo-rary repository of items that have been deleted from the desktop, from the list of favorites, and from the file system generally. The bin stores items until they are permanently deleted (by emptying the bin) or are restored to their original places. This is clearly an improvement on the old DOS way of doing things, where an "erase *filename*" sent the named file into oblivion (from where a restore was at best difficult, even if one had the tools).

My Documents

The My Documents folder serves the purpose of having a default location from where Notepad, WordPad and other utility func-tions can open files—and to which the files are saved, by default.

While this is a useful concept, the designers must have stopped to have a cup of coffee then forgotten to return to the task at hand—else they never really bothered to consult any users when they came up with this concept. I say that because it would have been nice had these utilities allowed one either to specify an alternative default folder or to have "remembered" the last place from which one opened a document.

This would save the many additional pointer actions required to navigate from the default "My Documents" folder to the root directory (often, but not necessarily C) then to the directory of choice. Windows is riddled with this kind of time-wasting functionality. The only way to get a utility like Notepad to return to the same directory as before is to do a "save as" then open additional files in the same instance of Notepad (another instance of Notepad will default once again to the My Documents default). One also wonders why "save as" works this way, but not save.

As it is, I use the My Documents folder only as a temporary depository for files that I get off the Internet. All other documents are stored in their respective folders. Hence, having Windows utilities use My Documents as the default depository for all document files is both counter-intuitive and a waste of time.

My Computer

My Computer is one of the standard items on the desktop, though in XP it has been moved off the desktop to the Start menu alone where it has always been anyway. My Computer is used to explore the hardware and software of the machine. It is an alternative to Windows Explorer for exploring what's on the computer. It is also used to make changes to the default "Settings" of various hardware and software functions. Since it also includes access to the Control Panel, it is also used to specify new settings.

I do not intend to do an exhaustive analysis of this function, but simply to point out and discuss a few things that I think are deficient in it.

Discrepancies in Disk Data

The first thing to note is that there are discrepancies between what DOS, Windows Explorer, DriveSpace and My Computer indicate about the disk drives. I was never able to find any "help" explaining these discrepancies.

Just out of curiosity, I did a comparison on the disk used and free values as displayed on DOS, Explorer, My Computer, and DriveSpace. Here are the results. The first value is the capacity, the second is the amount used, and the third is the amount that is free.

- DriveSpace: 1.89GB, 1.22GB, 686MB
- DOS: None, 1.08GB, 715MB
- Explorer: 1.89GB, 1.22GB, 715MB
- My Computer: 1.89GB, 1.22GB, 686MB

I suppose there is a simple explanation for these discrepancies, but I couldn't find it. Needless to say, something simple like this lowers my confidence in the rest of the system—not that Windows needs any more confidence-lowering events.

The Design of My Computer

The design of My Computer is a development issue that is based on the inventory of items included in this category, how those items are grouped together, and the functions they perform.

The Main Menu

The My Computer main menu (list) displays the following items (plus or minus, depending on the set up):

- Floppy
- C
- D
- E
- Printers
- Control Panel
- Dial-Up Locations
- Scheduled Tasks
- Web Folders

Control Panel Menu

If you then select the Control Panel, which is a submenu of My Computer, you get another, larger set of items:

- Add New Hardware
- Add/Remove Programs
- Connection Helper
- Date/Time, Display
- Find Fast, Fonts
- Game Controller
- Internet Options
- Keyboard
- Modems
- Mouse

- Multimedia
- Network
- ODBC
- On Screen Display
- Passwords
- PC Card
- Regional Settings
- Sounds, System
- Telephony
- Users

These two windows give us an inventory of the functions performed through the My Computer utility.

Now, System Analysis 101, week one, teaches you to break down the tasks or functions to be performed into their "lowest" components; it also teaches you to subsequently group common functions together, then to give the functions appropriate names. A fourth maxim is to eliminate duplicates: do something one place.

Yet, if you look at the list of items in these two menus, you can see that there are duplications, there are functions that appear, at least in name to provide common functions, and there are items that have not been named appropriately.

The XP Control Panel Menu

Windows XP addresses this problem, somewhat, by providing a less cluttered top-level Control Panel menu for those who want it. The XP solution is to insert a higher-level menu that lists the "categories" into which the previous lists may be grouped. XP lists the following categories:

- Appearance and Themes
- Network and Internet Connections
- Add or Remove Programs
- Sound, Speech, and Audio Devices
- Performance and Maintenance
- Printers and Other Hardware
- User Accounts
- Date, Time, Language, and Regional Options
- Accessibility

There is still an option in the XP release to switch to the "Classic View," which means that a user can choose to view the Control Panel that we find in Windows 98 and in versions earlier than XP. So, the result is that another higher-level menu has been placed by XP "above" (this is an hierarchical menu after all) the mess of disparate items we found in earlier versions of Windows, but those who prefer the cluttered and messy view can still have their way.

The XP version of the Control Panel that Microsoft proclaims to be easier and simpler to use, in reality simply adds two more layers to the menu hierarchy without really resolving the under-lying problem. To make a real improvement to this process, something like the help system search function needs to be added to the Control Panel so that a user can enter a search phrase for the task desired and the system then goes directly to the function, without the user having to trace a multi-layered path through the menu hierarchy. This is done on XP, but in a way that suggests it is an add-on rather than a designed feature. The entire Control Panel and My Computer functions, in fact, need to be re-designed.

Duplications

On the main My Computer menu, there is a Printers item that is used to add new printers and display already defined printers. The first, if not the second, is a "control" function. Then under the Control Panel, defined as a place where one can make settings, the Printers item is again included. Why is the same item included both under the main menu and in a submenu?

Furthermore, the My Computer, Windows Explorer, and DriveSpace[7] functions can all be used to display information about the disk drives. Such duplications are not only unnecessary, but they are confusing. Which one is *the* best tool to use for disk information? If there are differences in the information provided, which one provides definitive information?

Wrongly Grouped Items

Or, consider that on the main menu of My Computer. You have Dialing Locations (for ISP numbers), Dial-up Phonebooks, and Internet Connections then under the Control Panel's sub menu you have Connection Helper, Internet Options, and Telephony.

I'd like to see a show of hand of those who have memorized the different functions these six items perform. None. I thought so. Now, a little design work would have at least divided these

---

7   The path is: Start menu I Programs I Accessories I System Tools I DriveSpace.

six items (found amongst two menus, a main menu and a sub-menu) could have been grouped together into one function, or into two (one for the Internet-related functions, and one into the telephone and dialing functions). In XP, these are grouped together under the "Network and Internet Connections" category, but remain as separate functions within the category.

Badly Named Items

Consider, further, that on the main menu there is a Printers item (that adds hardware to the system), then there is an Add New Hardware function on the Control Panel submenu that cannot be used to add a new printer.

Or, under the Control Panel submenu, you have a Display item and an On-Screen Display item. You have to access these items to learn that the Display item should have been called the Desktop Display item because that's what it is designed to handle, while the On-Screen Display should have been called simply the Volume Screen Display (after all, the desktop is an on-screen display). Similarly, the Users item should have been called Multiple Users.

I realize, of course, that the stuff in the My Computer item, and particularly the Control Panel, do not appear to have been "designed" but grew by accretion the way stalactites and stalag-mites grow, with bits and pieces being added with each release. But I also hasten to add that these growths will never amount to a beautiful natural column, but will continue to resemble spaghetti. In fact, the entire Windows enterprise has this character. It was never designed; it just grew.

Control Panel Functions

Up to this point, we have only spoken of the outward appearance of the My Computer item. In addition, there is the entire set of functions that the menu items are intended to perform. These functions are of two types: some are clear and obvious functions, while others require detailed technical knowledge of the internals of hardware or software peripherals. No differentiation is made between these two types of functions.

Unintended Consequences

One feature of these functions is that they interlace. A principal result of this is that making changes in the default settings often have unintended consequences and may modify the behavior and appearance of the entire desktop. Most users have learned through hard experience that unless absolutely required to leave the defaults in place. If defaults must be changed, make sure you have no pressing deadline, and call in the "technical support" troops.

Missing Controls

Another feature of the so-called Control Panel is that there are many things you should be able to control but cannot.

Volume Control Function

For example, the volume control function displays an on-screen set of vertical marks indicating the volume setting (fewer lines mean lower volume). However, sometimes the volume control disappears and the volume control of any selected media player will not raise or lower the volume. One must re-boot the computer and try again. In vain does one look to the Sounds item in the Control Panel for how to bring the on screen volume control back to visibility. The Volume item of the Quick Launch toolbar provides two items: Open Volume Controls and Adjust Audio Properties, but neither of these affects a "lost" volume control.

Keyboard Controls

Another example of a missing function is the Keyboard item on the Control Panel. Great idea! You can view and modify keyboard functions, you say to yourself, then you open the item and all you can do is change the speed and language—but what about changing the keys, say the function keys, or turning off those infernal shortcuts that you always hit when you're typing. So where does one change the function keys? Well, Compaq has added an Easy Access Button item to the Control Panel, but that just changes the Presario-specific pre-set functions.

We could try Help (this function should be called Good Luck!). Help shows a number of function key topics, all of them on how to display such and such using function keys. But it shows nothing on either making them inoperative or changing their function. So, Help is no help.

Redundant Controls

Another problem in the Control Panel is that it provides at least one item that should either be on the main menu of My Computer or deleted entirely because it is redundant. For example, the System item on the Control Panel is badly designed and badly named. It has four tabs:

- **General**. Displays general information about the computer (RAM, Registration)
- **Device Manager**. If viewing by type (the default), and you press the Properties button, a one-tab dialog is shown that displays an icon and the name of the item you selected. Wow! View by connection provides details that only a hardware geek or hacker would need or love. There is also a Remove button. I have not tried that, but I wonder what yoyo placed that item so that a user could remove things like disk drives, display adapters, ports, and bus controllers! Putting this sort of function here and making it available to any user is not good design.
- **Hardware Profile**. Use this to change the configuration for boot-up. Incredible!
- **Performance**. File System, Graphics, Virtual Memory

The only valid tab on the System item in Control Panel is the Performance tab. The rest of the "System" information should be on the main menu of My Computer as "General Information" and there should be a Performance item in Control Panel, even if only hardware experts should touch this item.

The Never-ending Re-boot Hassle

Yet another "feature" of Windows generally and of the Control Panel functions in particular is that you never know what's going to happen if you change the defaults, and if you do change some defaults, you **must** re-boot for the changes to take effect.

So, for example, if you select the Settings tab under the Display Properties item in Control Panel and want to change the Colors setting, upon Apply you get a message telling you that the effects may make some programs behave incorrectly—and anyway, you have to stop everything else you have been doing and re-boot the blessed machine before going on. Please raise your hands if you have not had to perform this idiotic procedure at least 100 times a year. This is a blasted waste of time: let's add this to the invoice Bill Gates should receive from the industry. At least one hour spent re-booting per person per week. That's 5 billion hours a year. At $20 per hour, this yields a bill of $100 billion to be sent to Mr. Gates. At this rate, Mr. Gates is going to have a negative net worth very shortly.

Evaluating Windows

Following this all too brief look at the Windows OS, we need to ask: Does it live up to its claims? How does Windows fare when evaluated in light of Microsoft's claims about it, and in light of our own experiences

Windows according to Microsoft

Recall that the aim of Windows is to provide a "natural, or intuitive, work environment for the user" by using a GUI that includes the WIMP features: windows, icons, menus, and pointing devices:

- First, the user is provided with a desktop that provides applications that are run in windows;

- Second, items are represented by icons instead of words;

- Third, commands are grouped together into presumably logical menus;

- Fourth, commands are entered with a "mouse" (or other pointing device) instead of a keyboard, permitting the use of one hand instead of two, for the most part.

Windows

The first aspect of Windows that Microsoft features in the WIMP system is windows. Like icons, I think that this feature is of negligible importance and value; it certainly is not revolutionary, nor is it an innovation. We have had menus long before Windows was thought of. And we have had windows, at least potentially, ever since the first CRT came on the scene, for after all a window is merely a frame on a screen.

What Windows has done with windows is something that we can appreciate, even if the idea is by no means revolutionary. Once the hardware technology developed, the ability to minimize (and thus instantly activate) application windows is a nice feature, as is the ability to resize windows dynamically.

Overall, I'd give the windows feature a B.

Icons instead of Text

The second of the features that windows technology introduced and Windows exploited and made widespread in the technology of computing was icons or graphical representations of text objects.

In my opinion, however, icons are of negligible importance. As we have seen, icons add nothing functional to the desktop or to menus or to any of the thousands (if not millions!) of application programs and web pages (that now number in the billions). We could delete all icons from the Windows experience and still have all the functionality. In fact, with the proliferation of icons

I would suggest that icons are a detriment, a hindrance to the Windows experience. The bitmaps, gifs and other graphic files used by Windows and other programs to depict icons take up a relatively negligible amount of space (about 10MB for about 600 such files for Windows on my system). For that, we get more clutter and only aesthetic (appearance) value.

I suppose that icons do not hurt anything, beyond being annoying and without functional benefit. If users feel the need for text plus pictures, so be it—but there should be no delusion about their functionality, however. I'd have to say that the only function of my desktop that I recognize through its icon is the MS-DOS window; every other function for me is recognizable only through the "text" associated with the icon. I wish I could delete just about all other icons, but Windows forces us to live with these infernal things. Perhaps other people do use their icons to identify items on the desktop. The only benefit I can think of having both text and icons together is that we thereby balance the left (verbal) and right (graphical) hemispheres of the brain.

In terms of benefits to the user that icons provide, I'd give icons a D.

Menus

I'm not sure that I'd go along with the idea that Windows added anything to the menu experience, however. I rather think that with Windows, menus took a step or two backward.

Recall the description of the Start menu that requires following the path (navigating the choices down levels) each time you want to make a selection. The "old" menu systems (of a decade or so ago) were fixed, and once one had displayed a menu (a set of choices from one to n), ending a selection returned to the menu so another choice could be made. Windows, however, is single-threaded in this regard. Windows introduced multi-tasking in the windows environment, but reduced a potential multi-tasking function in the old menu systems to a single-task system. This is not an improvement.

In addition, we have seen in the case of the My Computer and Control Panel functions that these menus are very badly designed and confusing to the user. Overall, the Windows menus deserve a D-.

Mouse Command Entry

The single most important feature of the Windows experience is the ability to run commands through one or two clicks of a button. This feature is, of course, based on the concept of a "stored command," akin to the single most important concept introduced at the birth of computing, the stored program (which is just a series of commands). By storing commands, including all of their various arguments, parameters, options, and flags, then allowing them to be run through a point and click technology is revolutionary (given what we were faced with before this).

With a one-handed point and click technology, users were freed from always having to use two hands to type in commands over and over again, using a syntax that required an open reference manual on every desk. Commands ceased with the point and click technology from being atomic entities and became "molecular"; ceased being stand-alone and became "subroutines" of the working environment.

In light of the pervasive use of this technology in the Windows environment, we would have to say that Windows is a resounding success. Improvements can, of course, be made to this fundamental "ostensive reference and run" technology. When speech interpretation technology can handle ostensive reference (pointing to or naming accurately) easily and reliably, the point and click technology will rise to a different level, but it will, at its root, still be the same thing as we have today. Give the folks an A for this.

Overall, however, the WIMP deserves a C-.

Natural and Intuitive Work Environment

Now we come to the real crux of the matter. Microsoft claims that the intention of developing a Windows GUI was (and is) to provide a natural or intuitive work environment for the user. Lacking any guidance on what these words mean, we provided an interpretation that involves the following aims:

- Minimize contact with the internals of the software
- Minimize the need for technical knowledge
- Minimize the need to search far and wide for commands (that is, optimize the use of logical menus)
- Optimize the availability of help information

Minimize contact with the internals of the software

Windows fails to distinguish between the different types of users that may use the Windows environment for work. At a very minimum, we can distinguish between technical users (administrators, programmers, support, and other geeks and hackers) and ordinary users (who could care less about the internal workings of Windows and just want to get their jobs done).

Windows conflates these two types of users by providing a wide, open system that can be messed with (and messed up by) technical and ordinary users alike. An ordinary, non-technical user who wishes to "explore" a Windows system can screw the system up royally in a very few minutes through any number of different utilities on the My Computer menu and submenus. Even geeks and hackers experience great apprehension (even dread) when they make changes to the system using the standard utilities, though possibly nothing quite like the apprehension they may experience when the changes they make are to any of the "sys" or "ini" files, much less any changes to executable files using a hex editor or getting into a file with the regedit editor.

Occasionally, Microsoft saw fit to warn the user that only the System Administrator should make any changes (for example, Control   Panel | System | Performance | Troubleshooting   or Virtual Memory), yet such a warning is not made at many other points when any change could potentially kill the system and make it unusable.

In general, Windows does not distinguish between a work environment and a development environment. Nor does it distinguish between innocuous changes (like the changing the Screen Saver or Background images) and the potentially disastrous changes (for example, using the Remove button under Control Panel | System | Device Manager).

Now, I happen to think that providing an "open" system is a positive feature of the Windows OS, but there should be a way to "close" the system for those without any need (or sufficient knowledge) to work with the internals, beyond simply telling ordinary users to keep their hands off or assigning passwords or locking certain files, all of which can soon become a pain in the butt.

In summary, instead of minimizing the user's contact with the internals of the Windows environment, Microsoft has maximized it. Hence, on this criterion of a "natural or intuitive" user interface, Windows does not succeed.

Minimize the need for technical knowledge

In the good old days of Fortran and Basic programs, users needed to know how to run a program (type in the name and press Enter/Return). Beyond that, a user needed to understand the "technical" language of the application, such as accounting or inventory control, but no one had to know anything about do loops, subroutines, or other features of the programming language.

All this changed with the introduction of the Windows environment. Not only did the user have to know the technical language of the application they wanted to use, but they had to learn a whole new vocabulary of the Windows-specific language and its assortment of disciplines and sub-disciplines. Just to work within the environment, one has to learn terms such as active window, browse, control, dialog box, driver, folder, jump, link, path, pointer, profile, protocol, taskbar, toolbar, and many others.

Similarly, if a user wishes to customize or personalize their windows environment, they have to learn the technical language of numerous sub-disciplines. Here are some examples from Control Panel | Display.

- To customize the background, you need to know what an HTML document is, and what pictures are (bmp, gif) so one could create one not on the list.

- To customize the appearance, one needs to know what a "scheme" is (some combination of color, size, and format).

- To customize effects, one needs to know what it means to "animate" windows, menus and lists. Also, how many ordinary users have the foggiest idea what it means to "smooth the edges of screen fonts"?

These examples are taken from one of the simplest of the Control Panel functions. Consider what an ordinary user is faced with if they should wish to customize something like the virtual scrolling of the active window (under Mouse | Scrolling), where it takes a while to find out what the options are, then to experiment with the options. Even more demanding is the Advanced tab under Control Panel | Internet Options.

Evaluation? Windows does nothing to minimize the need for technical knowledge; in fact, it augments it.

Minimize the need to search far and wide for commands

Well, this is a mixed bag. Certainly, the most-used commands are on the desktop, so there's no doubt that this criterion has been fulfilled in this sense. Navigating the "major" functions is easy enough in most cases.

However, a major problem in the Windows scheme of things (using the term scheme here to refer to the position and placement of items within it) is that the categorization (or grouping) of functions is not always that obvious or natural (or intuitive).

Consider, for example, the matter of the volume controls for the CD-ROM. If one wants to locate this function, the "natural" place to look, assuming one knows in the first place that the function is under the Control Panel (which is under My Computer) is to look for something associated with Sounds. However, there's nothing there. So, the next option might be

Multi-Media. Under the CD-ROM tab, there is a volume control function, but this has no effect on the display of the volume controls on the screen, so one has to look under On-Screen Display to find the controls for volume control. Natural? I don't think so.

Let's try a simple task: removing items from the Quick Launch toolbar at the bottom of the desktop screen (default position). My Quick Launch is set up (by default) so that there are items on the left (next to the Start button), a section in the middle showing items currently open (such as Microsoft Word), then another set of items on the right side of the Quick Launch toolbar.

Since there are several items that are both on the right and left sides of the QL, I want to remove those duplicate items from the left side. I select an item, right-click and select Delete from the dropdown menu. Quick and easy. No problem.

Now, I want to remove some items from the right side Quick Launch toolbar. I select an item, but this time I do not get a pull down menu with a Delete function, but an item-specific menu (with no Delete function).

OK, why is the right side different from the left side of the same toolbar? Well, then, let's right-click on an empty space on the right side Quick Launch and see what we get. We get a tabbed dialog with the title of Toolbar Properties. OK, Tab 1 is for taskbar options like the icon size, whether or not time should be shown, and whether or not the taskbar should be always on top. Well, those options are already set, so let's try Tab 2.

Tab 2 is Start Menu Programs. OK, what's the relationship between the Quick Launch and the Start menu? Are the Quick Launch and Start menus one and the same thing? OK, well let's try one. Scroll down the list and I find that there's no correlation between the items on the right side Quick Launch and the list of items in the Start menu, so I back out of that trail. OK, then, let's try the help system. Over to the Start button and open Help; type Quick, and there is a Quick Launch toolbar topic; click; three subtopics display; click Putting toolbars where you want them…Blah, blah, blah, but nothing about deleting items on the toolbar. I open and read the other two topics. Nada.

By this time, I have spent fifteen minutes creating a drive image of my computer so I can restore if things go haywire (as is to be expected when using Windows); and I have now spent another 15 minutes trying to perform a simple task. No luck. No information available. So, I shall forget the exercise and just leave everything as is.

So, can you find commands when you need them under Windows? Fat chance. Good Luck, Charlie. The user is left to the mercy of whatever happens on Windows.

Optimize the availability of help information

I think we've already answered this question. I have yet to ever find information about anything I'm interested in knowing about, though I will admit that I have often found interesting discussions about topics in which I have no immediate interest.

Conclusion

One of the problems with (or is it features of?) Windows, one that is apparent to anyone who has used the system for more than five minutes, is that it was apparently never designed, but just grew topsy-turvy like in a helter-skelter way. Windows was just slapped together with spaghetti "design" and little attention to its audience (of users). For over a decade that Windows has been in existence, no one apparently ever sat down and asked the design questions needed to develop a well-designed system. Functions are just slapped onto an existing product, and out comes a new release. This is the case whether or not one is speaking of Windows 95 or Windows XP.

For these reasons, one cannot expect to find a logical menu system under Windows. Logic had nothing to do with the design; why should it have anything to do with the menus? In all likelihood, different teams of developers worked on different features of the system, with little integrated communication among them, so all parts of the system are not coherently integrated and standardized: some parts have context-help, others do not; some parts are well-designed, while others appear as mere hacks. More importantly, the concept of simplicity, particularly as applied to developing shallow menu systems has no place at Microsoft.

There is an apocryphal story in the industry to the effect that Microsoft (or whatever company one is not working for at the time) uses the first release just to get to market, the second release to do beta testing, and then gets it right on the third try. This is a mere self-serving myth, however. Microsoft has had over fifteen years and about eight releases (maybe more) of the Windows product—and it is still hopeless. Microsoft will never get Windows right if it continues to develop it the way it has in the past.

The only hope is that Microsoft one day will throw away all of the source code for Windows and do a complete re-design and re-development of the product. Microsoft needs to begin the user-interface analysis all over again. It needs to ask questions like: What do people want to use a computer for? Are icons really of value? What types of menus may most effectively be used in different places on the system? How can we improve the use of ostensive devices like the mouse? Is the point and click device the best we can do? Would some technology (other than the mouse or the WIMP factors) improve the usability of the computer?

Microsoft claims that XP is a brand new product. Contrary to that propaganda, however, Windows is still Windows—and Windows is still badly designed.

Chapter 4

Word for Windows

This chapter considers the Microsoft Word for Windows 2000 product, Version 9.6.2720. The chapter, like the entire book, is written using this product.

Word Processing

I know that many people regard VisiCalc, the first spreadsheet, as the killer application of the early days of personal computing, but to me that distinction is and always will be held by word processors—even those as primitive as the good old EDLIN in MS-DOS.

The Old Typewriter Days

No one can forget what it was like to be a writer (or a secretary) before the days of the word processor. Letters—and any other document form—had to be typed and retyped and retyped ad nauseam until they were satisfactory. The manuscript for an article or a book might go through several complete iterations before being submitted to a publisher—and perhaps several more before the thing was accepted for typesetting, which was entirely beyond one's responsibility or knowledge. Illustrations had to depend on picture or graphic designers.

Advent of the Word Processor

Then came the personal computers and their built-in word processors—electronic versions of the typewriter.

And everything changed for every writer.

You could write and revise a million times, if you wanted, all on the same "sheet" of paper (the screen and the file into which documents were saved), then you could send the document to a printer that did all the real "printing" work (of putting marks on pieces of paper).

Over the years, simple word processors have turned into entire document publishing systems so that one person can do all of the work that once required a multitude of people (writers, editors, typesetters, graphics designers, to mention but a few). Regardless of Windows, the word processor has transformed the writing life.

My Use of Word Processors

I have been using electronic word processors for many years. Beginning with the powerful Waterloo Script system that worked on the IBM 360 and 370 mainframes, and continuing on through the variety of word processing and "publishing" systems available today—MS Word, FrameMaker, WordPerfect, and others—I have used them all at some time or another. Some are better than other for some purposes, but all have these built-in capabilities of writer, editor, spell-checker, grammar checking, formatting, exporting in different formats (for hardcopy, electronic viewing, and HTML for the web) and so on.

I have used MS Word since its inception, I think at least since Windows 3.1, at any rate. I have used Word for letters, articles, books, and everything in between. It has, of course, evolved over the years. New and powerful capabilities have been added. I think, particularly, of the table-creation and formatting capabilities that alone warrant the cost of the product. On the other hand, it has some features that annoyed me when the product first appeared—and still annoy me today. And some of the features contained in the version that I am using now (Word 2000, Version 9) are downright annoying and infuriating.

MS Word and the Flow of Work

MS Word is a killer application all right, but it also exemplifies to perfection some of the key failures of all Microsoft software. In the following sections, I want to look at MS Word through the eyes of one user—and tell you what I think its strengths and deficiencies are.

I will be looking at Word from the viewpoint of the process of using Word. All work involves a process, a flow of activities. I want to look at Word not just as a set of tools or functions that are available on the application (the way stock is available in a warehouse), but as a set of tools or functions that have a **context** and contribute to or detract from the flow of work.

Capabilities a Writer Needs and Wants

Before looking at Word features and capabilities, we need to at least define the writing process (the flow of work) so we will have a "natural," inductive foil or standard against which to consider the features of Word.

Well, the first thing one needs is a "desktop" that is cleared for action, and contains within easy access the things one needs to perform the writing task. The "frame" of the Word application, what is visible when one opens a new document constitutes this desktop.

Next, one need something to write with and write upon, and some way of identifying the one or more "pages" that will constitute the document to distinguish it from other documents. One also needs different ways of making these marks upon the "paper". If multiple authors may be involved, one needs collaborative tools. One also needs to keep track of when marks were made (given the possibility of different versions).

As one proceeds with the writing tasks, one needs handy ways of formatting and re-formatting material, sending it to a "printer" (virtual or real) to be able to see the finished product. If there are different outputs (the document composed for various media), then one also needs to be able to test these as well.

Assuming that the document is to be published in some form and made available to readers upon demand, then all of the usual publishing functions need to be handy as well.

Set up of the Writing Environment

In this section, we are concerned with an understanding of the way the writing environment is set up.

Document Identification

The first set of things I would like to do include identifying the document and pointing to the new directory (or folder) from which the document is to be opened and to which it is to be saved (including the save frequency).

One of the features of Word is a tabbed dialog that is used to store information about a specific document. This feature is accessed from File | Properties. It would have been nice had the designers called this the Document Properties, but we can let that pass since they at least include the name of the file in the title area of the dialog.

I'll start by noting something about the document. I pull down the File menu and see a Properties item, so I open that. Enter a Title and subject under the Summary tab then skip the rest.

Whether rightly or wrongly, one of my habits is to Save As an existing document that is like a new document I want to develop. When the new "saved as" document is created or updated, Word will automatically store some information associated with it, including changes to the name of the template attached to it, readability statistics, and the like.

But there is one thing it will not change—the original title of the document. Neither the File | Properties | Summary | Title nor the Contents Title are changed by Word, but left as it. Unless one remembers to update these properties, a document could carry along with it the original title; a document with the title of "The

Great Virtues," could have had as its original title something unrelated. This problem should be corrected in Word.

File Locations

Next, I'll specify the file locations. Naturally, I look under the File menu, but there's nothing there. So, I have to go wandering around. Finally, under Tools | Options, I find a File Locations tab. Now, why isn't that tab under the File menu instead of under the Tools menu (for the love of Mike, all these things are tools and options)?

Anyway, I want to record where the files for **this** document (or project) are to be saved, but the first item in the File Locations tab says "Documents" rather than document, so it seems that this file location is a global setting, but I want a specific setting for **this** document, not a general setting for all documents (I don't have such a thing). But no, Microsoft has no way of specifying the open and save file locations for this specific document, just for Word as a whole. Not good!

So the effect is that I'm going to have to open and save **this** document under one file location, then remember to re-set that location if I open another document for another project, and so on back and forth. When I no doubt forget to change the file location, I'll be saving **this** document sometimes under its proper location and sometimes under some other document's location. This is not a helpful feature.

Well, when perplexed, read the documentation, so maybe the help system can supply some clarification on this. Well, there is a topic on changing the default working folder, but you can change it for Word or for Office only (at least that's what the topics say), but I want to change it for a document, not for every document using every instance of Word.

Well, maybe there's some information about this on the Microsoft network itself. In fact, I find one under the list of the most frequently asked questions about Word 2000. Under the topic "How to Change the default file name and location"[8]

I'm informed that there are two methods that can be used. One is to assign the document to a particular dot file, a particular template, then set the options for the template to the file locations I want.

However, this just moves the question one step backwards. Does this mean that I have to assign that template to each document I want to open in file location X, then a different template to every document I want to open from folder Y? If so, then I have to remember to update both templates if I want them to be the same on every other factor, except for the file locations option. This violates the standard rule of programming—make any routine you have to use at several locations into a subroutine, so you change one subroutine rather than every instance of the routine whenever you want to change something.

Save Options

Well let me set the save frequency and other values. Since the Save and Save As functions are under the File menu, I'll look there first for the save options, but No, the save options are under the Tools | Options | Save tab. This is another bad design move by Microsoft.

---

8   See support.microsoft.com/support/kb/articles/q212/3/86.asp.

Oops, I had to change something in that previous paragraph and the damn thing overtyped what I wrote instead of inserting the new word that I wanted to add. OK, so where is the editing mode set? Under the Edit menu, I'll bet. No, that would be too obvious. I'll bet it's under the Tools I Options menu. And so it is. Overtype mode must be the default (who writes this way?), so I unmark that option, click OK, and return to my tasks.

Text Background

Another thing is that I like to make my screen easy on my eyes, so, for example, I like Black text on a yellow background. I'd suppose that option must be under Tools I Options—everything else is, instead of under page setup (File menu) or the Edit menu, or the View menu, which make logical sense, but not so Microsoft could tell.

OK, so I look under the View, then the Edit tabs under Tools I Options, but my black-on-yellow option isn't there. Finally, I locate it under the General tab, but there's only a white-on-blue. So either you take the black on white or the white on blue—or nothing.

One can, of course, go to Format I Background and change the background color—but that effect is negated as soon as you change the document view—or open another document—so it's not even a session-level function.

Disabling Shortcuts

Oops again. Now I'm suddenly typing stuff in italics, as you can see. But I didn't want italics. I must have inadvertently pressed CTRL+I or some other one of their infernal shortcuts—which are useful if you want them, but not if you don't. So, can I turn off the shortcut?

Fifteen minutes of perusing the Tools I Options tabs shows nothing related to shortcuts.

So, let me try the help. My document window shrinks and instead of putting the help system on top, it places it beside the restored (shrunken) window. OK, I guess that's a feature. So, I search the Keyword list and find Shortcut and Shortcut Menu, but when I do a search for related topics, help returns zero each time. So, why include a keyword in a help system if you have no associated topics?

I turn to the various other possible keywords that could be involved: Disable, Turn Off, Hide (or Show). Many associated topics, but nothing related to shortcuts (like disabling shortcuts). Another great user-centered feature, eh? Microsoft, like all other companies, likes to talk about user-centered design and development, but this is just lip service without any substance. I'll have to live with mistakenly enabling of shortcuts.

Spacing after Periods

Another thing I like to do (and adopted as a standard for many years when doing technical documentation) is to add two spaces between a period and the start of the next sentence. This is something that must be done automatically; if it isn't and you have to do it manually, there will always be periods you miss and the formatting will be screwed up.

So, I open the help system and type "spacing." The help system displays many related topics. I read a number of them, but I cannot set the spacing between sentences. Another bummer.

Using the Help System

It's become apparent that I'm going to be using the help system as I go along on this project, though I'm not all that confident that the help system is going to be that much help, but we'll see.

In this version of Word, Microsoft has changed the behavior of the system so that when you access help, here is what happens:

- The maximized window is restored to about 60 percent on the left

- The help system main window is superimposed on the right 60 percent

- The help system then informs you of the ways you can get help while you work

I don't find this way of placing the help system to be particularly useful or "user friendly," but I can live with it. I suppose there is some way of customizing this feature, but I won't bother looking for it until such a time as this setup becomes exceedingly annoying. Also, once the help system has been opened one time and the ways you can get help read and understood, why keep repeating it every time help is accessed?

Another, related feature of the help system is that one is never sure which side of the screen it will show up on—it could be the left or the right side. This is somewhat disconcerting. This should be a user-set preference.

Setting up Toolbars

The toolbar on Word 2000 is the one we've all come to expect, except that it's become so cluttered that submenus have been added at several points. I've removed most of these items, since I do not expect to use them right away.

I also find most of the icons to be space wasters that have absolutely no use. Except for a few icons that have been around for so long—open, save, cut, paste, copy, and undo—all the rest have no intuitive or obvious meaning and so could just as easily be left off the toolbar.

The standard alignment functions as well as the bold-italics-underline (BIU) functions are all right. I notice that there are layout icons in the lower left-hand corner, but with no obvious way to eliminate them. Since they're unobtrusive, I guess they can be left as is.

This is another of Word's tiresome features—it is documentation intensive. There is hardly a function that one can do without searching through the interminably long and generally useless help system topics.

Marking up the Document

Now that we have set up the writing environment in Word, we can turn to the actual task of writing.

Writing at its most basic level is simply marking up a medium (screen, paper) with marks of various kinds (usually words or graphics or pictures) arranged in a certain way.

Writing Methods

Some writers prefer to begin with an outline that is then fleshed out; others prefer to write first and then find the outline after the fact. The method selected may also depend on the kind of writing involved—a technical treatise is best outlined ahead of time, while a novel's outline may emerge only while in the process of writing. Word provides the tools that both types of writers need: outlining tools that may be used to lay out a document before the content is developed as well as the straightforward tools needed to just start developing content on a blank screen.

Word and the Writing Process

One of the nicest features in Word is the auto-correction feature whereby common typos are corrected as one types. Word comes with a few standard templates for this and others that can be added by the user.

Also nice is to have a document spell-checked as one types. Spelling mistakes or words of unknown correctness are flagged as one goes along. In addition, if I misspell the word dragon as "dragan" the latter is flagged as a mistake. If I then place the cursor over the misspelled word and access Tools I Spelling and Grammar (or click the appropriate icon on the toolbar) the misspelled word can be corrected in place (by clicking Change) and can also be added to the list of terms to be auto-corrected. However, it is annoying that one has to access the Tools I Spelling and Grammar menu twice to accomplish this feat, once to make the change and again to add the word to the auto-correct list.

User-Defined Tools Options

There are some things that one does **not** want to be flagged as spelling mistakes (for example, "Tools I Options"). If you go to Tools I Spelling and Grammar I Options, a Spelling and Grammar options box is displayed, but on it there is no way to add an option, such as the one above, to the list of items that should or should not be flagged. Adding each such path to a custom dictionary is too much of a pain to bother considering. One should be able to inform the application that some types of word, such as those with a " | " are to be ignored.

What Microsoft should have considered in its design of its "options" menu generally and certainly for the spelling and grammar options is a way to add user-defined "ignore" options. Instead of the application assisting the writer, the writer is obliged to adapt to the application's deficiencies.

Annoying Expanding Menus

Another feature of Word is the use of expanding menus.

If I open the any menu on the application window and do not make a selection within a few seconds—I think it's five—the menu expands. Now, I went looking for where I had seen this setting (I thought it was under Tools | Options), but I did not find it. Never mind. The point is that Microsoft should have included a user-settable option to set the time gap between opening a menu and when the menu expands. As it is, the Options selection on the Tools menu is the fifth option on the minimal menu, but the sixteenth item on the expanded menu. This use of expanding menus is annoying and distracting.

I know, I know. I **can** change the menu system, but that's just another time-consuming bother. I'd like to be able to either set the number of seconds before the menu expands—or, better, eliminate the minimal menus altogether. Besides, the frequency with which I use a menu option should never be a criterion for determining if an item should appear on a collapsed menu list. What would happen were automobile manufacturers to have used this approach when determining whether or not the brakes should be activated on a car.

Splitting URLs

So far the line by line formatting hasn't been troubled by compound terms like Tools | Options, but somewhere along the way they are going to be when the paths become longer than two of three words separated by the pipe (|). However, already problematic are the URLs that I will be using to reference the sources of some of my comments (particularly those about Microsoft!). Since many of these URLs are long and are not split-able (the default logic), I'm going to face problems. I need a way to specify that compound "words" like URLs can be split at some point (for example, at the | or at the /).

Searching for help topics with the word "split" in them reveals a great many topics, but none applicable to this problem. One solution is to select each URL I'll end up with and change the font size so it fits (maybe); but this is not a good standard and is not reliable.

Another solution is to put each URL at the start of a line and in a footnote or endnote. But this is a bit too pedantic and will not work if the URL is really, really long. Yet another solution is to insert a hard break at the point where a URL could be broken, but this is the worst solution because a change in font size or output type (for example, XHTML) would create formatting problems.

The Wandering Cursor

Another problem I've suddenly discovered is that the position of the cursor on the screen as I type is not the same as the position of the cursor as the mouse sees it. Thus if I decide to return to a previous line or paragraph to make an insertion, I have to go "find" the mouse cursor and bring it to the place where I want to make a change. This is the problem of the "wandering cursor."

Ideally, of course, the screen cursor and the mouse cursor should be locked together so that when I reach for the mouse I can move the cursor from its current position (the end of the last word I typed) to the position where I want to make a change. However, that is not how Word works.

Wandering Pictures

A related problem is that the pictures I have imbedded in this document never remain where I place them from editing session to session. Sometimes when I open the document, all the pictures are where I placed them—centered. At other times, one or more but rarely if ever all of the pictures have been left shifted. This is another example of what I call the unreliability of Word. It is completely unacceptable to have a word processor change formatting of its own accord.

Resuming Editing or Writing

The more I write, the more I wonder if any writer was ever involved in designing this "writing" tool, or were only techies (who generally hate writing and writers with a passion) involved?

When you are writing, you generally like to open the document you're working on and have it go to the end of the document so you can resume writing. But, no, Word always opens the document to the first page. Brilliant.

So, let's see if there's an option for this. As usual, we go to Tools I Options and the Edit tab. Nada. OK, maybe there's an "Open" option. Well, there are Open options; you can open a file as a copy or in read-only mode, but nothing about "opening **to**" (for example, open to start, open to end).

All right then let's look in the help system (not that it has ever been of help so far). Still no help from help. Searching the topics on "open" yields hundreds of topics, but none even remotely related to opening a document "to" some part of it (like the last line you typed).

So, this has to be done as a manual function using CTRL+END (or SHIFT+F5 if I want to move to the last insertion point). I suppose I have to put this into a macro that executes when a file is opened—something I'll leave for another day when I have nothing better to do.

Find Dialog is Irrational

One of the worst dialogs in Word is the Find dialog. Quite often you want to look for a word, do some work, then look for another word or look for the same word again. To keep the Find function open, you can try to move the dialog to some unused part of the screen or you can just close it. If you move it to one part of the screen, you will probably have to move it again, and again while you work. If you close it that means you have to open it again when you need it. A far simpler approach would be to provide a minimize capability on the dialog.

Find is also a pain to work with when you use it continually. When searching for the same word over and over again, the dialog box keeps moving around. This is a pure distraction and unhelpful. If the box keeps moving around, then you have to keep moving the pointer to "Find Next." Sometimes the dialog moves out of the way so you can see the next word, but sometimes it covers the word so you have to move the dialog out of the way. It would help were the dialog a wide, horizontal one that stayed put. An excessive number of pointer moves have to be made to use this function.

Auto-format Needs Correction

If you provide a function, please make sure that it works. The auto-correct function is a nice one, but it doesn't work correctly all of the time—just some of the time, which is worse than none of the time.

Take the hyphen (—). When you're entering text and use a double dash, the program will automatically change it to a hyphen . But suppose you actually want a double dash and not a hyphen? There needs to be a way to define a letter, word, phrase or sentence as a "literal" that is not to be changed by the auto-correct or auto-format functions.

Opening Multiple Instances of Word

If you open one instance of Word and subsequently open a document within it, all you can do is close the document or open another document. The previously opened document remains "under" the newly opened document.

I find this not to be suitable if I want to work with two different kinds of documents simultaneously, so I usually open a second (or third…) instance of word so I can minimize, restore or maximize them, as the case may be. One very annoying feature of this process is that the second (or third…) instance of Word always opens in a restored size—and has to be maximized before opening a document in it. It would help to open all instances of Word in a maximized window.

The Overtype Mode Default

A related annoyance is that while the first instance of Word will remember that I detest the Overtype mode (set in Tools | Options | Edit), the second instance invariably uses the default Overtype mode. There should be some way, other than templates, to set global characteristics of the Word environment. I've wasted a considerable amount of time overtyping when I meant to insert.

In addition, there is something terribly wrong with an application that changes the editing mode (invariably from insert to overtype) within sessions of the same instance of Word, while editing the same document. Just today, on one document (this one), I have had to change the editing mode back from overtype to insert several times when for some unknown reason Word decides to change the mode from my normal insert mode back to the overtype mode. There must be a shortcut involved! Also involved is a dumb design!

Unexpected Renumbering of Lists

As I was going through this particular document file, I found that all of my numbered lists had been renumbered, without asking or expecting, into one long numbered list that spanned several headings. This is unacceptable. Once a list is numbered, it should **never** be renumbered by the application itself. And numbered lists should **never** span two headings. A new heading should automatically mark the end of a numbered list.

This is another example of how Word is unreliable—Word cannot be counted upon to behave properly. If you have to check what your word processor does to make sure it did what you wanted it to do, you've wasted your time and money on a useless piece of crap.

Adding Comments to the Text

Word does not have, but needs, a way of inserting comments directly into the text, which are not to be printed. It would be helpful if one could add comments about ideas, additions, missing items and so on right in the text. All programming languages and major league level word processing systems (on mainframe computers, for example) have such capabilities—and what is Word but another programming language for writers?

Comments could be considered as a field, which can be seen but are not processed unless specifically requested (like the index or table of contents). Comments should be visible when editing but not processed for printing unless requested.

Formatting with Style Templates

The writing process, I know, differs from writer to writer (and software documentation from department to department), but the one I follow is to develop rough first drafts without paying any attention to the format of the document, then in the editing phase of the process, I apply a style template and adjust the rough text to conform to it. So at this point, I need to find and adjust or develop a template for this book, then apply it to what I have already written.

What I want to do is very simple. I want to:

- Find a template whose elements (headings, table of contents, etc.) match or can be adapted to the style I want for the book

- Globally change the template to the font I want to use

- Attach the template to the document whose first, rough draft I have completed

- Reformat the rough draft to match the template

Create a Template

Now I need to create a template. Since it makes sense to stand on the shoulders of others and not re-invent the wheel, I'll start by looking for an existing template.

Try Office Assistant

The Office Assistant is a new breed of help that is called an "expert agent." Windows XP is filled with these agents, so we may expect future versions of Word to have even more of them.

- I try Help and open the office assistant.

- OK, then what?

- Try a right click. It gives me some options including hide the assistant. No, this doesn't do it.

- So, try a left click. The assistant displays a list of options about file conversions, which have nothing to do with anything. It also tells me to type in a question and do a search.

- OK, I type in "create a template for a book," then click Search. This time the assistant displays a list with the heading "What would you like to do?" and lists a set of irrelevant options (none of them have anything to do with templates). Well, the assistant has glassy eyes with huge irises; I assume the fellow is on drugs; time to hide this idiot from view.

Try Microsoft Word Help

All right, let's try again. This time I'll try Help | Microsoft Word Help.

Once again, the office assistant displays. Instead of a question, I'll just type in "Templates" and click Search.

OK, this time the response is better (the assistant can deal with one word, but not with a question, it seems); at least one option is to "Create a document template." I click on that topic and the help window displays. Now we're getting somewhere.

To create a document template, I learn, I can use one of two methods. The second mentioned method, to find a template similar to the one I want to create seems right on. I write down the instructions (As an alternative, I guess I could leave the help open or print the text).

Look for a Template

Using the instructions in the previously accessed help message, I proceed to look for a template.

- I click File | New, then check "Create a new template".

- A tabbed dialog displays showing a variety of available templates. There is a "Pleading Wizard" for Legal Pleadings (I'm not going to touch that one!); ten letters and faxes; four memos; seven for other documents (mainly resumes); eight for web pages; three for reports; and four for publications (brochure, directory, manual, and thesis). Thirty-seven templates, and not one that even closely-resembles what I want.

- So, I return to the "General" tab and select "Blank Document," because it is clear that I'm going to have to create my own template.

- I click OK, then Save As and give it a name, then click Save. The new template is saved in C:/windows/application date/Microsoft/templates so it will be available among the general templates I can select for a new document.

- Word shows "Test" (the name of the template) in the title area of word, but gives no other indication that Test is a template. I have to set the Windows-level file extension visibility to on if I want to see the extensions of open document files.

- What now?

- Well, it seems I need some more help, so it's back to Help and do a search on Templates. The first topic is "Modify a document template." I'll try that.

Modify the Template

So, I read the "Modify a document template" topic. It tells me that I can open the template, change aspects of it then save it— but it **never** tells me **how** I am to change the template.

I check another topic, "About templates." No help on how to change templates there, though now I know there are so-called "global" templates (the Normal template among them; so why didn't they call it Global.dot?) and document-specific templates. So, it appears that I'm going to have to figure out on my own how to change a template.

- I begin with the File menu. Nothing there.

- Edit menu? Nada. View?...Insert?...Format?...Nada.

- Tools menu? Ah! There's a "Templates and Add ins" option. Try that. Not at all obvious or intuitive what this topic is supposed to do. Context help is useless.

- OK, back to the Format menu and try the "Styles" option. OK, this dialog displays a list of what look like document elements (called styles, for God only knows what reason). Maybe this is where document template elements are defined.

It appears you can select a style (element) and see how it's defined. Most of these elements use a font I do not want. I want to change the font for all elements in the template. How do I do that? Do I have to do a "Modify" on each, and every element? Yuk! There must be a better way...Ah, there's a "Default Paragraph" style. Maybe if I change that it'll make a "global" change. However, when this element is selected the Modify button is blanked out.

So, I check a number of different elements (styles) and most of them are based on "Normal" plus additional definitions. So, perhaps if I change the font for Normal I'll also change the font for all elements based on Normal. Yes! That's it! I modify the Normal font, request that this be added to the template, and click OK. Now, many elements have had their fonts changed by this action—but not all. Some of them, like Comment Reference, I'll leave as is because I don't think I'll be using them. When I'm through, I save the template.

Now I need to attach the template to the document.

Attach the Template to the Document

To attach the template to the document, I proceed as follows:

- I open the rough document that I wish to format (and re-format) in the style of my new template.

- I open Tools | Templates and Add-Ins.

- I enter the name of the template, then click Attach, then Close the dialog.

- Immediately, the font in the document is changed to the font in the template.

Reformat Rough Draft to Match Template

I now want to proceed to change the headings, add notes and footnotes, and make other editing changes to the rough draft of the document to which I've now attached the new template.

Back to Straight Quotation Marks

However, there is an unexpected consequence: those nice curly quotation marks have been replaced by straight quotation marks. The same result occurred for the apostrophe.

What happened here? I open Format | Autoformat | Options and the "Replace" options is checked to have straight quotes replaced by smart quotes—but precisely the opposite has happened. (I know that at least the auto-correct function to replace dashes by a hyphen still works, so it's not as if the whole auto-correct function is not working.) I haven't a clue as to the problem here.

It took me several weeks to find out that while the default font, Times New Roman, substitutes curly quotes for straight quotes naturally, the font I had selected to use for this document, Arial, did not have curly quotes. Now, it would be nice had the documentation mentioned that some fonts, such as x, y, and z, do not perform the substitution of curly quotes for straight quotes. Thus, to make the substitution a global option when it applies only to selected fonts is bad design.

Whoops—Headers and Footers Problem

I went to attach a bullet to a single line. Immediately each line in the entire document was re-formatted with a bullet. I opened Edit | Undo and got the option to undo automatically update styles. I clicked that, and the bullets were taken off each line but left on the one line I wanted, but suddenly the header and footer spaces took up a third of the page each and the document expanded in the number of pages by 300 percent.

All attempts to open the View | Header and Footer functions or the Format | Style functions for the header and footer showed no place to modify the amount of room left at the top and bottom (visible with a dashed box when the View | Header and Footer selection is open).

This could not be a problem in the template since all the other documents I formatted using it are all right. After trying for close to an hour to find a way out of this, I simply closed the file and left to have a cigarette—and to roundly question the maternal and paternal ancestors of Microsoft. When I opened the document again after that, the headers and footers were still screwed up. Something's screwed with the "automatically update styles" function; I bet Microsoft knows about this and refers to it not as a screw up, but as a "known issue" (a rose or a bug by any other name...).

How am I going to resolve this problem? Well, the first thing I did was open Tools I Options I View and turn all field codes, formatting marks, and text boundaries on. Once this was done, the document showed three unnecessary and unwanted paragraph markers in the headers and footers. I opened View I Headers and Footers, then deleted these paragraph markers on the first couple of pages—and zoom, the document reformatted itself with the correct header and footer sizes. But why this problem occurred in the first place is something I do not know.

Modifying Template and Document

As I go along, I have the document template open in one instance of Word and the document itself open in another instance because I like to change styles as I go along. It is, however, annoying to have to close the Word instance in which the document is open each time I change and update the template for the template changes to take effect.

I can update my bank balance from here to anywhere in the world, but I can't get Word to update template changes automatically when both document and template are and open sitting right here on the same computer.

I suppose I could update the template from within the document, but I find that even with "Update styles automatically" set to Yes, the style changes made in one document do not get carried over when I open another document with the same template attached.

No Mass Change on Styles

As I am going along, I see that there is a format style in the document that I want to change. I want to keep the current style name, but change all items with that style to a style of a different name.

The Edit | Replace function will not work for something like this. I need a way of selecting all items with style x and replace them with style y. The Edit | Select All function will not work; speaking of which, we need an edit select function other than Select All.

After searching wide and far for some way to accomplish this, I realize that there is no way to do this other than by touching each and every item in the document currently with style x and changing it to style y. This is an unacceptable feature.

I am constantly reminded of the pack of BS that Microsoft put into its document introducing Word 2000, for example: "Word can take the tedium out of writing, and let you focus on putting your ideas into words..."

At every turn in Word, the lie is put to the idea that using Windows and Windows-type applications enhances productivity over what was provided by command line user interfaces. Changing a style in an SGML or XHTML document is a keystroke or two away, while making the change in Word is a tedious process requiring a manual editing procedure. This is true at so many points in Word that I have to wonder if the developers ever used a "real" word processor before they tried to develop Word.

Inability to Print Styles

When doing XHTML work, one can construct CSS style sheets and view them as normal text. A similar capability exists in BookMaster, troff, SGML and related word processing systems—but not Word.

There is no way to print the different styles that belong to a named template and look at them as text strings. There is thus no way to compare different template styles. The styles can be displayed only in fragments (the font format, the numbering format, the paragraph format, etc.) at a time. This is a serious deficiency in an already deficient application.

Publishing Tools

The processing flow of writing brings us now to the use of publishing tools. When a book has been written and edited, the next step is to assemble its various parts into a whole.

Creating Master Documents

As a general rule, any document over twenty pages or having multiple component parts, such as chapters or sections, is better done if the individual components are developed separately, then assembled into a whole when the "publishing" step approaches. This is the way a manufacturing process is set up: queue the completed parts then assemble them (kit them) according to some recipe (a procedure).

First, however, I need some information about assembling separate documents into a book.

- I access Help | Microsoft Word Help.

- I type in the keyword "master" to look for information related to master documents.

- The system responds with three related keywords: master, master document, and master view.

- Interested in what a master view is, I select that topic. It concerns e-mail replies. Not what I was looking for.

- I retype "master" in the search area. The system refuses the word and inserts "master view," and the "master document" keyword is no longer in the keyword list.

- I have to close help and re-open it to be able to re-type "master" and this time select the master document topic.

Cool, eh?

Methods of Assembling Master Documents

In the case of a book, there are two principal ways in which the assembly process can proceed. One way is to create a small, driver-type master document that points to the files (components) that compose it. So, for example, one could have a master file that looks like this when displayed:

title.doc

chap1.doc

chap2.doc

A second way to assemble a book is to create a new document and copy (or insert) the individual components into it.

If the first method is selected, then the individual components can be changed and edited whenever desired, but when the master document is processed the components are merged so that tables of contents and indexes are performed for the entire assembly—and any changes made to the individual components are reflected in the assembled document.

If the second method of assembly (copying each part into a master document) is used, then changes can be made only to the master document and no longer to the individual components. This can be a real pain in the butt if the writer decides to make mass changes in content or structure to one of the individual components, since changing a small file (for a component) is far easier than changing a huge file (containing the entire book).

Word's Concept of the Master Document

Word's concept of the master document appears to be a combination of the two methods of document creation described above. To create a master document in Word, one creates a new document—using the same template as used by the individual parts (which has many problems attendant to it)—by inserting component documents by name into the master document. To edit a subdocument, one must open the master document in outline view then edit the subdocument from there.

One should also be able to edit any subdocument by itself, without opening the master document. However, Word appears to store information about each of the subdocuments in the master so that changes made to subdocuments "outside" of the master document tend to screw up the master document. This is an unacceptable feature. Subdocuments should be editable from within the master document as well as individually.

Creating the Master Document

I followed the above procedure and created the master document without any problem. However, when I later went to insert another subdocument between two existing subdocuments, Word made the insertion at the end of one subdocument instead of between subdocuments.

Editing the Master Document

However, now I have some serious problems. I would put the following into a numbered list, but I cannot because when I click the numbering tool, it changes everything to a heading 3 in the rest of the document. So, in paragraph form, here is what I was trying to do after I had created the master document.

First, I found a list whose single-spacing I decided to change.

Second, I selected the entire list and went to change the style from List 2 to Normal.

Third, I then went to re-apply the numbering to the "normalized" list.

Fourth, no change occurred.

Fifth, I selected each line individually and then clicked the numbering tool. This time, instead of a number, the line was changed to a heading 3.

Sixth, fortunately, there is an undo function. So at this point, it becomes obvious that Word does things on its own. I am spending too much time redoing things over and over again that Word undoes.

Wunderbar!

Index Dialog is not Usable

Another dialog that is very badly designed is the Indexing dialog. As provided, it is a square non-modal dialog that remains open after one has made an entry so that additional entries can be made. That feature is all right, but the square blocks most of the screen so one has to be constantly moving it around, trying to get it out of the way so the screen can be seen and read.

The dialog needs two design changes. One is to make it so the dialog can be minimized and restored when needed. The other design change is to make the dialog a wide but shallow one so it fits over the menu bar area of the screen rather than over the screen itself.

Intermediate Page Printing

The printing process leaves some key automated functions out. If you specify on Page Setup | Layout that a section (for instance, a chapter) is to start on an odd page, then one would "naturally" or intuitively assume that when printing the application will know that if a previous section ends on an odd page a blank even page needs to be printed before starting the next chapter.

Word is "smart" enough to do this, but it does not know enough to print the header and footer—and page number—on the blank, intermediate page. The result is a number of "missing" pages between chapters. I'm going to have to manually insert these missing pages.

Changing Book Sizes

Since the book is to be published in a 9x6 size, while I'm developing it initially in the usual 8.5x11 size, I thought I would develop two master documents, one for each size. I changed the page size for one master document from the usual set of margins to the margins that would apply for a book smaller than the usual 8.5x11.

The body text and headings changed all right, but the headers and footers did not carry over. This means, essentially, that if you change the normal size to another size (larger or smaller), you have to change the header and footer styles as well! This is a dumb concept. I am used to using IBM BookMaster, troff, or IBM SGML where such carryovers are simply a keystroke or two away from implementation. Having to use an application like Word is therefore a step backward—make that several steps backward.

One should be able to change the page size, headers and footers, and so on from some document properties dialog. This Word is Mickey Mouse stuff.

Changing Views

Well, now that the individual components of this book are getting in shape, I want to see what the different views of the document provide. So far, I have viewed this specific chapter in outline, print, and normal views. Now I'd like to see it in a Web page view.

OK, that seems to be OK, so I'll now switch between the different views just to get an idea for what happens to the document under the different views.

All went well until I went into Print view, then catastrophe struck.

The base font for the document (as specified in the template) is Arial. However, when I displayed the document in Print view, the font changed from Arial to something else (though the style still says Arial)—and I can't get the document to revert to the base font (Arial) in Print view.

What is to be done?

Clearly, if I cannot get the Print view to change to the proper font, I will not be able to get a proper print out of the master document. Copying the document in normal view and saving it in that view, then changing to Print view has no effect. The solution is to copy the file in normal view and then open a new document with the template attached then paste the normal view in. This worked fine. But the problem still remains as to why the document was stuck in an abnormal font when in Print view.

One needs reliability and dependability in a word processor. If one has to constantly check and re-check to make sure the application does what you expect, you might as well use a typewriter.

Document Statistics Incompatible

Another example of unreliability comes from the functions and data supplied by the Spelling and Grammar function on the Tools menu.

First, on the matter of functions, it seems odd that the Tools menu supplies a Spelling and Grammar Option and a Word Count option, but does not supply a Readability Statistics option. To obtain a word count, you simply go to Tools | Word Count, but to obtain a Readability Statistics you have to open Spelling and Grammar then process the entire document before the function displays those statistics when it is through.

Second, the data supplied by various functions on the Tools menu is inconsistent. The word count supplied by Readability Statistics is 11,934; the Tools I Word Count function supplies 11,762; and 11,764 is supplied when the "Include Footnotes and End Notes" option is checked.

Now, which of these three different values am I to believe?

Contents and Index Pages

To get a table of contents and index for an entire book, you obviously need a master document (or place the entire book into a single file). However, since you obtain either one by imbedding a command (TOC or INDEX) at the point where you want the contents or index, you end up with a single line for each in the source, and the index or contents are generated only when you go to print (or print preview).

The problem with this is that one generally includes a header and footer on index and contents pages, but if the application only inserts a single line to cause these to be generated (at print time), there is no way to get multiple-page contents or indexes with the proper headers and footers—except manually. If this is automation, give me a pen and paper.

This is utterly ridiculous. The application should be smart enough to "know" how long the index and contents will be and generate the appropriate headers and footers. This capability has been around on non-Word word processing systems since Adam (or at least twenty years).

Contents and Index Data Unobtainable

Another thing that I need to be able to do for a "publishable" book is to produce a table of contents and an index without page numbers.

My first attempt to create a table of contents without page numbers was to insert the TOC command (Insert menu) at the top of the document, then generate a print preview that I could copy and paste. It turns out that you cannot copy a print preview page.

All right, the second attempt was to display the document in outline view showing only the headers in the collapsed document. I did this and did a copy on the displayed headers, but when I pasted them into a new document, the entire document file was copied—not just the headings as I had wanted.

So, what are my options at this point? I can copy the document (leaving the original untouched) and the cut all the text out leaving only the headings. This manually intensive chore should not have to be done were I dealing with a real word processor made by and for professionals, but it appears that I have no other option. Doing this for the index as well is going to be excruciating.

Changing Headers and Footers

A serious deficiency in Word is the inability to set headers and footers in the master document. In serious word processors like the ones already mentioned (BookMaster, SGML, etc.) one can specify a header for an entire manuscript on one line in something like "<header>$chapter$page" and the footer as something like "<footer>$book", where the $ prefix indicates a variable.

In Word, however, one must first access each document file in a book, then access the View I Headers and Footers and make the appropriate entries. If you change your mind and decide to modify or eliminate the headers and footers, or their style, you have to do the same things over again. This is a colossal waste of time.

From Master to Merged Document

After struggling with the Word "master" document for several days, I've come to realize that the master document is not really capable of providing a finished product, but is an intermediate step between individual documents and a book. The master document is useful while one is in the process of building a book, but must eventually be replaced by a single file that holds all individual documents, not as linked files that can be manipulated from within a master document but as an integral part of a single document.

Like Word itself, the master document is really only a toy—it cannot be used to produce a finished document that is ready for publication.

Evaluating Microsoft Word for Windows

Since we would expect that an application developed for Windows would aim to provide the same user-experience as Windows, we will use the same criteria to evaluate Word as we used for Windows.

Windows according to Microsoft

Recall that according to Microsoft itself, the aim of Windows is to provide a "natural, or intuitive, work environment for the user" by using a GUI that includes the WIMP features: windows, icons, menus, and pointing devices:

- First, the user is provides with a desktop that provides applications that are run in windows.

- Second, commands are executed by pointing to icons instead of typing;

- Third, commands are grouped together into logical menus;

- Fourth, commands are entered with a "mouse" instead of a keyboard, permitting the use of one hand instead of two, for the most part.

Our expectation is that these features of Windows apply also to applications like Word for Windows and all other Windows-based applications.

Word's Application Window

All Windows applications that I know of begin by opening an "Application Window" that provides the principal work environment for the application and from which all subsidiary utilities are accessed.

Multiple Instances of Word

For some applications, multiple windows can be open at the same time, each with an instance of the application running in it.

Other applications, like Word, allow only one application instance to be running in any instance of Word. So, if you want to view multiple documents at the same time, you have to open multiple instances of Word. I suppose this is OK, except that I find that even with 128Megs of RAM, Windows often informs me that I have to close one or more of those instances if I want to run some utility (like Control Panel).

I also find nothing appealing in the way Word opens a second instance of Word in a restored window. Why? Why not maximize the second (or third...) instance of the Word application window from the start?

The Exit Control

If you open an instance of Word then open a document within it, Word displays a small exit button (x) beneath the window's usual exit button (in the upper right-hand corner). If you then close the open document, the smaller exit button goes away. If, however, you open a document in Word then open another document in the same instance of Word, the smaller exit button (x) disappears and the second open document is closed using the large exit button (X).

Would someone please explain the brilliant reasoning involved in this feature of Word? Why not display a multitude of smaller exit buttons for each open document? There's enough space to show at least twenty open documents, though I'd be very surprised to learn that anyone ever opens twenty documents at one time. The open documents could be listed from left to right, one small exit button for each.

Generally, the use of windows in Word is not user-friendly.

Icons in Word

The second of the features that Windows technology introduced and made widespread in the technology of computing was icons, graphical representations of text objects. The Word application includes a host of icons: icons on the toolbar, icons on some but not all menu items, icons within subsidiary utilities, icons for file types, and so on and on and on—ad nauseam.

Some menu items have icons, while others do not. There's an icon for Save but not for Save as; there's an icon for Insert Comment, but not for Insert page number or picture; and so on. If you're going to use icons, use them consistently; otherwise don't use them at all. It appears to be quite arbitrary which items have icons and which do not.

Some icons are quite intuitive and helpful: cut, bullets, numbered lists, move left or right, alignment of text, and columns are great. But most of the others are far from intuitive, and even after ten plus years of looking at them, they have no meaning or use for me—icons like New, Open, all the icons on the View and Insert menus, most on the Format menu, and so on are just clutter.

Just what is it that you people are trying to do with these icons? Please give me a clue. Maybe just keep the graphics people gainfully employed?

In sum, just as in the case of the Windows use of icons, I find the Word use of icons to be only partially worthwhile. The only one that really saves me time is the scissors (cut); the rest I could live without.

Menus

It appears to be a standard that all Windows utilities (such as WordPad, Notepad, Explorer, and Internet Explorer) are given the same "fixed" set of menus (File, Edit, and Help) with all other menus being customizable to the utility. If the application may include more than one window open (one active, the rest inactive) at the same time, a Window menu is also included in the application.

Word fits this mold. It has the standard menus (File, Edit, Window, Help) as well as application-specific menus (View, Insert, Format, Tools, and Table). Having developed Windows applications, I know that the application-specific menus are as easy to develop as typing their names into a list.

One reason, I suppose, that the Windows application environment defined this standard of always having the File, Edit, Windows, and Help menus on the application window is so that users would be able to expect the "same" experience when using different Windows applications from different vendors. The File menu would always be used for Save and Save As, for Print functions and the like; the Edit menu would always include cut and paste functions, and so on. This is a commendable aim.

However, the aim is not realized if functions that belong logically (semantically, if not syntactically) under a menu are not included under that menu. The aim is also not realized if menus that should logically exist are absent from the application.

Tools Options Menu

We have seen that somewhat as an after-thought, Word includes an Options menu under Tools. There are tabs in the Options dialog for a wide variety of functions:

- View (Display of view and formatting marks)
- General (Background color, measurements)
- Edit (Mode, picture editor, paragraph style)
- Print (Print options, includes)
- Save (Embedded fonts, save as, file sharing)
- Spelling and Grammar (Options)
- File Locations (Global settings)
- Compatibility (Dozens of possibilities)
- User Information (Name and address)
- Track Changes (How changes are to be tracked)

It is quite obvious that the View and Edit options belong under the View and Edit menus, respectively; the Print options belong either with the print options under the File menu or under a separate menu; the Save options under the File menu or under a separate pull-down.

There is already a Spelling and Grammar item under the Tools menu, and the options for this feature should be included there. File locations belong under the File menu. User Information belongs with the Properties under the File menu, or elsewhere. Compatibility is all right where it is, though it could have been placed under a Compatibility menu item on the Edit menu. Track Changes belongs under the Properties item under the File menu. General Options could have been included under the File menu.

Furthermore, some of the items that are placed under some of these menus should have been included as single items on the menus where they logically belong. To change the editing mode from overtype (the default) to insert, for example, now requires a four-step process (Tools I Options I Edit and OK). This should be a two-step process (Edit, Click). Similarly, the background feature on the Tools I Options menu is incompatible with the similar function under Format I Background. The two functions, which are now dissimilar, should have been made one function on the View menu. And numerous items on the Tools I Options I Compatibility tab should have been included elsewhere.

In short, Tools I Options is a lazy piece of work that is incompatible with the stated aims of Microsoft to provide users with usable software.

Template Menus

The same can be said for the functions related to templates. As we have seen, the template-related menu items are scattered all over the place—and even where they exist, there is little intuitive or natural sense to their placement. I certainly am not about to do Microsoft's work for them and tell them how to arrange their menus in a logical way. My point is that someone should be doing this at Microsoft—but isn't.

Menu Depth

Unlike Windows, Word tends to have shallower menu structures than Windows. In many cases, one can perform a task (find a command) by tracing through three or four levels. However, there are some functions that are placed into a three or four-step menu path that should be placed at a much shallower level and other functions that are placed at a shallow level that could just as logically be placed at a deeper level.

Selecting the paragraph spacing for a document is a four-step process (Format I Paragraph I Indents and Spacing I Spacing). Selecting the editing mode (overtype or insert) is a four-step process (Tools I Options I Edit I Overtype off or on). These two functions should be at a shallower level.

On the other hand, some commands that could just as well be deep within the menu structure are shallow. For example, specifying the language for a document, something one would do once and never again is a three-step process (Tools I Language I Set Language) and changing case, a rare occurrence, is a two-step process (Format I Change Case).

Mouse Command Entry

There's not much to say here. Like Windows, Word uses the mouse for point-and-click execution of commands. Other than always having to re-position the mouse cursor so it coincides with the real point of action, the ostensive mode of command execution is far better than the old command line mode. What benefit Word gives us with the standard Windows point-and-click mode of command execution, however, is taken away many times over by a klutzy command processor that does not always work reliably or predictably.

Overall Evaluation of the Natural or Intuitive Interface

All software development companies love to talk about the user. They use words like "user friendliness" or "human-centered design" and sprinkle references to "human factors" throughout their software literature. Yet, the eyes of all users glaze over when we hear these terms and phrases—because we know that they are all BS. There isn't a single software company in the world that has produced user-centered software. Why is this so?

That is so because you cannot "factor" in the human user the way you factor in a number in a linear equation. To produce software that takes account of the user, you cannot factor the user in—the user must be the central element of all design and development work. Human or user-centered software is software that begins and ends with knowledge about human cognitive, affective, and motor abilities—and the nature of human work. Human-centered software is software that provides tools that the user needs to do work—not tools that the developers think they need. Human-centered software provides means to user ends—not tools as ends in themselves.

Software that is user-centered must not only differentiate between different types of users, but must also focus exclusively on how those human users do their work. To develop a word processing application does not involve, as Microsoft and so many other companies seem to think, focusing on the capabilities of "word processing" in some environment or programming language. Rather, it involves starting the entire design process by asking: How may any user work to perform this task, and how may the computer aid in the process?

Microsoft has not produced a natural or intuitive user interface to the processing of words via Word because it has not focused on this question. Word provides us with a wide variety of functions that could just as well be stored in a warehouse and pulled off the shelf. It does not provide the writer with an environment to assist in the processing of words—it provides tools that the computer thinks we could or should use, and in the order in which the computer or some technical person who has never performed the task at hand determines. Other than open and save, there's nothing natural or intuitive in Word.

Overall Evaluation of Word

For documents of less than twenty pages or so in length, Word is probably as good as any other word processor. If you have longer or more complex documents using non-standard styles, you're better off with an old-fashioned command line interface using IBM BookMaster, troff, Runoff, or GML-based systems like SGML or XHTML—or with a well-designed application like WordPerfect.

My overall feeling for Word is that it is tiresome and loath-some. It cannot do many things a writer needs to do, and many of the things it can do it does either badly or unreliably. Word is not a dependable application; it cannot be counted upon to do anything other than behave badly. It is a paradigm case of a user-unfriendly application. It is badly specified; displays no evidence of having performed any requirements analysis; shows mediocre if not unintelligible design and as implemented it unreliable, with a tendency to do things on its own accord.

Word has no sense, no feeling for the flow of writing work. The developers can add all the menu items they want; they can add all the expert agents like Office Assistant that they want. They can add icons, they can add functions, they can offer views of all kinds—but that will not change the fact that of all Windows type applications that I have ever used, Word is by far the worst. I realize that I have only touched a few of the functions in Word, but like an egg, you don't have to eat the whole thing to know that it's rotten.

Chapter 5

Microsoft Network

This chapter describes the Microsoft Network, Version 6.10.0016.1619, which is accessible via the "http://www.msn.com" URL. Though the Net platform is the rose of Microsoft network, it should be remembered that the heart of the net is Windows XP, which explains why XP and the MSN Explorer, described below, have the same look and feel.

The Historical Context

As we speak, Microsoft is engaged in a head-to-head combat with AOL to dominate the Internet service provider industry. At the current time (late 2001), AOL has about a four to one advantage over MSN (30+ million to 6+million) in its subscriber base. Both currently charge more-or-less the same for their ISP services, though the AOL home page is accessible only to subscribers, while the MSN home page is accessible to everyone, subscriber or not, who has an ISP.

AOL provides numerous services in addition to acting as a portal to other web sites. The Microsoft strategy seems to be to use MSN as a central site for access to the wide range of Microsoft products as well as Internet services. Instead of competing by providing a portal to the World Wide Web, Microsoft wants to compete with all others by providing a wide range of services and software that enable people to perform tasks on the Internet.

Home Page Architecture

The architectural styles used in constructing the home pages for Web sites are few in number. Just as the variety of DNA is described as the interaction of a small number of fundamental forces or interactions, in this case four, so Web page architecture has only a few fundamental styles. Some sites use one style throughout their pages, while others use different styles for different purposes throughout the site.

One fundamental decision that Web page architects have to make is which style to use for the opening, main, or welcome page.

The Highway Model

One style is the highway model, probably the most frequently used style, and the one that exploits the hypertext basis of the Web in a minimal or limited way.

In this model, a Web page is one long unidirectional highway starting where you open the URL and can theoretically extend forever (and some pages I've seen seem to). The information provided by this model is arranged as one long series of points, like a printed book, and is accessed serially.[9]

The Shuttle Model

Another style is the shuttle or looping model, where you go back and forth between two points (load and end of page), with stops (links) in between. Online newspapers are fond of using this style.

The shuttle and the highway models are alike; they differ over the length of the page and in their use of categories. The highway model uses a minimum number of categories, rarely more than one, and each item (link) is of the same type as all other links. You can think of the highway model as one long list of items, which are alike. The shuttle model, on the other hand, generally uses a small number of categories under which it lists items belonging to each. Thus, a news site will have local, national, and international news categories, for example.

The Central Hub Model

Another model is the central hub model, where you enter to display a fixed view from which all links are made and to which all links return. Though there are a few sites that I have seen that use an approximation to a central hub model, only AOL, and Microsoft MSN Explorer use this model consistently. It consists of a fixed page wrapped around a window to access subsidiary functions.

---

9   For an example, see www.aldaily.com.

The British Garden Model

Another model of home page architecture is the British garden style. In this style, you're never quite sure where you are, where you're going, or what you'll see, but it might still be interesting. This is a commonly used style. MSN uses this architecture in its home page.

The MSN Web Site

The MSN website is accessible in a variety of ways. Here we are only concerned with browser access.

Accessing MSN

The MSN web site is accessible from two types of browsers: (1) The Internet Explorer (or Navigator, or other) browser, and (2) via the MSN Explorer.

Accessing MSN through Internet Explorer

If you already have an ISP and Internet Explorer is used as a browser to access MSN, the MSN website opens, naturally, within IE, to display the MSN "home" page. The normal Internet Explorer functions are still available to you, because Internet Explorer is the "wrapper" for the home page, as it is for any other home page that you open. The architecture of this mode of access to the web site is the "shuttle"; to view the contents of the site, you have to scroll up and down.

Accessing MSN through MSN Explorer

Another way of accessing MSN is through the MSN Explorer. The MSN Explorer is a fixed wrapper (using the central hub model) that curls around the home page or any other selected page and provides a fixed view (and experience) from which one navigates the Web. This wrapper is centered on the user, or what Microsoft has determined is the user, and is intended to provide the user with a unified personal experience.

MSN Explorer uses the top and left sides of the maximized screen to provide its wrapper then displays selections (such as URLs and mail functions) either within a fixed sub-window, or by opening a new window (via the More Choices | New Window option). Though re-sizeable, these new windows open initially to a size about one-quarter the size of the screen, which to me is not attractive.

One has to wonder what Microsoft is attempting to convey by the use of such a model for the wrapper. As it is, the wrapper appears to take up about thirty percent of the entire screen, leaving the other seventy percent for the rest of the Internet. I suppose one reason for this extensive amount of screen space devoted to a wrapper (a portal to the Internet) is simply ego—a huge ego. It could be that Microsoft believes it is like the rooster that thinks the sun rises each day to listen to him crow. The impression given is that the "rest" of the Internet is not as important as the wrapper for the MSN.

Top of Explorer Wrapper

The top of the fixed wrapper provides a limited set of simple and intuitive icons for back, forward, home, mail, favorites, buddies, chat, money, shopping and music.

This is the first time in my experience of Microsoft software that I can honestly say that icons make sense and are an attractive addition to the window. All other uses of icons in Windows, Word and in other software that I will not talk about here are useless and hindrances to a good experience with the software.

In MSN Explorer, Version 6.10 please note, we have a simple and elegant wrapper and a well-designed use of icons. I'm not saying that the icons are useful in the sense that their functions could not be performed without them. Far from it. Words could serve just as well as the icons. It's just that the icons are "pretty"—they have an aesthetic appeal, which is one of the criteria for a pleasant user interface.

Command Set

Immediately below the major service icons, is a URL open area and a small set of commands (or menus of commands). You can Go, Stop, Print the active page, Refresh, and can select some of the usual File, Edit, Window and Help menu commands from the More Choices menu:

You can open a new window, cut, paste and copy, select all, review settings, and access the MSN Explorer Help.

Left Side of the Wrapper

On the left-hand side of the wrapper, there are a few words (Calendar, Stocks, Communities, Search, City Guide) and a large icon for the built-in music player that allows you to access music without opening another window.

This left side, too, is elegant in its simplicity. Whether or not these are the main attractions for me or any other individual is something else altogether. For my part, I'd replace Stocks with News (but this is something I can do if and when I personalize the browser).

One feature of this left-hand side of the wrapper is the icon with two greater-than characters (>>). You can minimize this side of the wrapper (actually it shrinks it about 80 percent) and so give the active window greater width.

Oddly enough, the MSN home page does not take advantage of this extra space, but simply leaves the extra (white) space visible in the window.

Evaluation of the Wrapper

As an idea, the wrapper is a good one. It puts a fixed point of reference as the central visual and auditory (MSN Explorer welcomes logins with a few spoken words) experience of MSN.

The MSN Explorer wrapper is currently simple and quite elegant—but takes up too much space on the screen. I say "currently simple" because as I remember AOL's early wrapper was also simple and elegant, but by version 7.0, AOL's wrapper had become overloaded with an excessive number of features that required too much effort to use. My sense is that Microsoft has a tendency (see Windows, see Word) to overburden (that is, clutter) its software with unnecessary or badly designed menus and lists of commands (or features), so I fully expect later versions of MSN Explorer to follow this trend. For the moment, however, it is simple and elegant—maybe too much so, since many functions found in normal browsers are missing.

On the other hand, the amount of space taken up by the wrapper on the screen is unnecessary and egoistical. The wrapper could be shrunk to one-tenth the size without losing any of its effectiveness. Certainly, the left side of the wrapper should be eliminated (pushed up into the header area) so as to leave more room for the display of the MSN home and other pages.

Minimizing Open Pages

One annoying feature of the MSN Explorer experience is that it is no longer possible to minimize a page that is opened within the wrapper's window. If you want to minimize (and thus keep accessible) an open page, you must use the More Choices | New Window option to open the URL in a new window, then minimize that new window. This new window is only about one-quarter the size of the original window so additional mouse actions are required to re-size it (in addition to opening it). I suppose the intention is to discourage access to home pages other than MSN's, which simply defeats the purpose of using MSN Explorer as a portal to the Internet.

Importing Favorites

One of the things that Microsoft touts as an example of how easy MSN Explorer is to use is that one can import Favorites from Internet Explorer to MSN Explorer. Well, I tried this function and it was not at all satisfactory. First, my Favorites were imported in reverse order (last first). Second, only a small subset of my Internet Explorer favorites was imported. If I then clicked the "more" option on the bottom of the favorites drop down menu, this took me to the Organize your favorites window instead of to more favorites.

To try to correct the problem, I had to delete all existing favorites and try the import again. That had the same result. Some more work needs to be done on this function, fellows.

Unable to Play Music

One of the enticements Microsoft uses to attract users to MSN Explorer is that one can listen to rich media while browsing the Web without opening up separate programs or windows.

Naturally, I tried this function. I selected my favorite Internet radio station URL that plays the world's greatest music[10] and waited and waited and waited while MSN Explorer told me it was Tuning In—but nothing ever happened. I had to open the URL from Internet Explorer as usual before I heard a single note. This problem may be because the URL requires a different media player—but, then, MSN Explorer should be able to handle things like that by loading a different media player.[11]

---

10 See kompamania.com that plays the incomparable Kompa music of Haiti (select the Kompa channel).

11 I believe this deficiency is a conscious decision that has something to do with Microsoft and some of its competitors. Such childishness is intolerable.

The MSN Home Page

Whether accessed via Internet Explorer or MSN Explorer, the MSN home page is the same in both cases, except that under Internet Explorer the page is visible maximized, while in ME it is visible in a sub-window of the MSN Explorer wrapper. By using the aforementioned >> icon, you can shrink the left-side of the wrapper and give the home page or any other open page more room to display in. Unfortunately, the MSN home page remains the same size as before, so that shrinking the left side simply opens up a column of white space on the right side of the sub-window.

On opening the MSN web site via either Internet Explorer or Explorer, one is presented by a screen that presents only a partial view of MSN offerings. To view the entire home page requires one to scroll down several screens; on hand-held devices, the views may be even more limited, and will require a great deal more scrolling.

The MSN home page suffers from a lack of design, categorization, and the placement of content. One would think that a company with as much loose change lying around as Microsoft would be able to afford a few content designers and put them to productive use.

While MSN Explorer uses the central hub architecture for the "wrapper", both MSN Explorer and Internet Explorer display a home page that is built on the shuttle architecture for navigation, and on the English Garden architecture for its content.

Shuttle Navigation

To navigate the MSN home page, you have to get on the shuttle; you must scroll up and down looking for the things you want to access. One result of this use of the shuttle architecture is that it is impossible to gain an "overview" or grand picture of MSN offerings through one window or screen. Instead of using a "big picture" window to show us the sights, it's as if we have to peer around columns (as at a baseball game) or as if when sitting anywhere in a football stadium one only had a partial view of the entire field.

A consequence of this is that one does not have access to all MSN offerings at one time. One is constantly scrolling the home page, up and down (and sideways, in some cases) to find the service that one is looking for.

The English Garden Architecture of Content

In addition, the design of this home page leaves a great deal to be desired as a design experience.

The navigation of the home page, as noted above, is via the shuttle architecture; the design of the content of the page is more akin, however, to the English garden. I say that because there is little rhyme or reason to the placement of the content, no categorization that has any intuitive intelligibility. Stuff is placed all over, and some stuff, like the weather or personalization features (which require the use of the Passport feature, if it can be called a feature, as distinct from a pain) are placed several times on different areas of the page (no doubt so you'll not forget or you'll get so annoyed you'll sign up).

All of the personalization features, like changing the content of sections, or removing them altogether, require the use of cookies, which is a questionable design requirement: suppose you don't want to allow cookies, for privacy reasons? Yes, of course, you can set an Internet option so that you are prompted each time a cookie is used, but think of the pain of having to say yes to half a dozen dialog boxes requesting permission to use cookies when all you want to do is change the colors on the screen.

Help System

The help system for MSN comes in two flavors, one for Internet Explorer and one for Explorer.

Internet Explorer Help

Accessing help from Internet Explorer opens a window that displays an "Overview" of help as consisting of four categories:

- Help Topics
- FAQ
- Technical Support
- Contacting Microsoft

MSN Explorer Help

If you access Help from MSN Explorer, on the other hand, you receive a window that shows the top ten topics of interest, the first of which is the usual help topics. The remaining top ten topics concern things like changing account passwords and the like. It isn't as obvious from this window as it is from the Internet

Explorer help how to contact Microsoft or how to get technical support (which is included among the items listed on the left side of the window).

Home Page Help

The help for the home page itself also leaves a lot to be desired. I suspect this is because the writers are as confused as I am about the design and layout of the content.

For the life of me, I can't after spending hours checking out the home page find any intelligible (or intelligent) order in the way content is positioned. I think there may have been an original intention to provide some order for the help speaks of "quick links" which are directly under the special headlines, and "service links" which are placed on the left side of the top of the window. This may be true of the lists of items placed at the very top of the home page, but after that, these differentiations cease to have any application—items are just thrown in left and right according to someone's whim of the moment.

Section Headings

The section headings are also of no help in finding any intelligible order. Some of these heading names are hilarious in the way they obscure rather than reveal:

- MSN Worth a Click (I assume this means the rest isn't worth a click?)
- Summer Travel
- Links and Resources (everything on the page is a link or resource, folks)

- Find and Share
- MSN Spotlight
- Interactive Highlights
- Today on MSN

Repetitive Content

There is also a lot of repetition. There are at least two links to the horoscope, four to automobiles, four or more to the personalization routines, three to the weather, five to shopping, and so on. Someone on the "content design" team must have a motor mouth or be working on some amphetamines. By the way, saying the same thing over and over and over again is a sign of insanity. Caveat Emptor.

Overall Feeling for the Home Page

Microsoft has a bad habit, one that we've seen in Windows as well as Word, to try to be all things to all people. The MSN home page is the result of this propensity: throw everything into the barrel, Willy-nilly, and maybe any one person will find at least one thing they like or want. This tendency to overload an application or a page with excessive content or features is one of the greatest weaknesses of the Microsoft software development architecture.

I rather suspect that the reason the home page content resembles an English garden is that Microsoft thinks that if there is no intelligible order, and no way of mapping the content, then everyone will have to look at everything every time they log in—and this means more exposure (not to say access time) on and for MSN.

However, this feature requires too much attention from the user, which is another feature of badly designed software. The content needs to be categorized and laid out in an intelligible way—and by this I do not mean the way the content is currently differentiated (by quick links, service links, local lookups, and so on). Content designers need to be hired and put to work to make this MSN home page an intelligible and worthwhile experience.

If an intelligible order is missing from a page, that makes it difficult to perform any work using it. Meaningful work flows from step to step. Intelligible work involves a flow of work steps. If an intelligible (and intelligent) order is missing from something like a home page, then no real work can be done with it and all of one's effort is expending just looking around randomly for things to do (and click).

The Search Function

MSN claims that one of the advantages of its Web site is the use of Alta Vista's "powerful" search engine.

As we all know, among the many weak links of the Internet (weaknesses like privacy, security, and so on), one of the weakest links is the search function. I have used just about all of the most highly touted search engines, and none of them are worth a damn. Oh, I do like the way Alta Vista (or MSN) adds sequential numbers to its display of the items that result from a search. However, I find it almost completely useless in the way it assembles result lists for searches. If one does a search on one word, I suppose one has to put up with the thousands of possible responses. However, when one word qualifies another, one would expect to find only items that at least match the two words in the say, top one hundred items.

The sequential order of items that are returned as a result of a search is also a problem. Different search engines (and their variants, like Web crawlers) often list items at the top of lists because of clever uses of "meta" tags in the HTML underlying Web pages or, in some cases, because of some monetary consideration. There is currently no objective criterion for why some pages are placed near the top of a list and others not.

The number of items returned is also a problem. I would like to see a show of the hands of those people who have actually plowed through and looked at the 7,720,830 items that my search function returned when I did a search on "time and space". Of what use is it to return millions of links? If I spent just ten seconds on each item, I'd need a entire year to browse each item—assuming my internet connection stayed up that long and I worked around 10 hours a day.

There is absolutely to reason to return anything more than the top 100 hits for a search. I know that the search engines use various methods to retrieve items—and that sites use a variety of different methods to get themselves into the top items in a list (not excluding monetary incentives and plain cheating). But there must be some way of separating the wheat from the chaff. Perhaps display hits by country or by age of site or by some other set of criteria.

A little over twenty years ago when I got into personal computing, one of the principal reasons for doing so was to be able to explore interconnections among databases on a worldwide scale.[12] The recent development of the XHTML and XML languages for the Internet may allow us someday to interconnect data from different Web pages, but for now we're limited to one page at a time viewing and no interconnectivity. Our search engines suffer from the same defect.

Evaluating Microsoft Network (MSN)

Microsoft's latest venture has been to extend the Windows interface into the Internet environment. Thought it was late (by a few years) in catching on to the market that AOL captured via its AOL portal, Microsoft is now hurrying to try to capture a share (the greatest share?) of the market for what is called the Internet market. While AOL wants to provide a portal into the Internet, Microsoft also wants to provide all of its software and services via the Internet.

MSN according to Microsoft

According to Microsoft, MSN provides "a single integrated experience that helps consumers get more from the Web." Using the best of Microsoft's Internet and other software (such as Hotmail), MSN, and particularly MSN Explorer, "is easy to use and personalize, and is designed to provide users with a refreshing experience."

Well, how does it do?

---

12 See Derek Kelly, "Applesaurus and the World Brain," *Creative Computing*, March 1981, 156-166. Now defunct, this magazine was at the time edited by Ted Nelson. Twenty years later, we're both waiting to see the promise of personal computers realized.

MSN's Application Window

All Windows applications that I know of begin by opening an "Application Window" that provides the principal work environment for the application and from which all subsidiary utilities are accessed.

As we have seen, the application window differs by the browser in which it is opened. If opened from within IE, only the MSN home page displays; if displayed from within MSN Explorer, which is also touted as a browser, the home page is wrapped within the MSN Explorer framework.

In the MSN Explorer, which serves as an ISP, e-mail agent, messenger and browser rolled into one, Microsoft seems to have moved away from the ever-expanding menu system of Windows to a sort of restricted command set architecture, though this may only be because they are beginning to try the "net" market.

Installing MSN Explorer

MSN requires that those who install the MSN Explorer use the Passport function to sign up and store their personal data on the MSN servers. At a time when concerns about privacy and about identity theft are quite high and Microsoft servers are constantly being hacked, this requirement is suspect. The Passport function, in particular has raised numerous industry concerns, particularly since it is so vulnerable to hackers.[13]

In addition, while the MSN Explorer's download and installation experience are well done and relatively painless (other

---

13 See www/avirubin.com/passport.html.

than having to use Passport), the MSN Explorer Terms of Use agreement gives everything to Microsoft and little, if anything to the user. The user is given a wide range of cautions about doing various and sundry things; Microsoft is excused from any responsibility for loss of personal data (that Passport requires) and is held blameless for all other possible sins of omission or commission by humans or the deity. You get to use e-mail, chat rooms, messenger services, shopping, and others services for free—but all at your own peril, not Microsoft's.

Icons in MSN

As we have seen throughout this consideration of Microsoft software, icons are a mainstay of Microsoft software systems and services. While I'll be the first to admit that the MSN butterfly is pretty (or aesthetically pleasing, if you prefer), and that the other icons on the MSN Explorer are attractive, they serve no unique or fundamental function that could not be served by words alone. Major battles are fought in the marketplace over icons, but I see this as much ado about nothing (other than brand recognition).

Menus in MSN

The menus of commands available under MSN differ according to the browser that is used.

MS Internet Explorer Like Windows

One of the advantages of opening MSN from within the Internet Explorer is that the "standard" Windows menus as well as the by-now expected Internet-related functions are available to the user.

For example, under IE, one can access the File menu and choose to work offline; one can also save pages. Using the View menu, one can see the HTML source code for a Web page or move to full screen; using the Tools menu, one can set Internet options.

MSN Explorer Omits Windows Functions

If, however, one opens MSN using MSN Explorer only a small subset of the usual Windows-IE menus are made available. Under MSN Explorer, there is no way to work offline because MSN Explorer is strictly an on-line utility. Similarly, there is no way to view the source HTML. Since all Internet Options are stored on the MSN network servers, there is no access to that function. However, since one does not download MSN Explorer in whole to one's computer (it remains on the Microsoft servers), one no longer needs to download updates (Microsoft does that on its servers).

While I think I understand some of the reasons why the MSN Explorer browser uses a restricted command set, it is somewhat unnerving to find that some of the neatest functions (like viewing the source) are missing. Has the concept of the "user" now being changed from the "everyone is a user" concept under Windows and Word to a concept that the Internet user is a novice?

The Natural or Intuitive Interface

Microsoft informs anyone who wishes to download their MSN Explorer that it is simple, easy and exciting to use, complete in its range of services, flexible, slick, and the world's most used portal to the Internet.

Marketing hype aside, is the user interface on the MSN site natural or intuitive?

If one is speaking of the home page, the answer has to be no. The home page is as natural as an English garden, if you like things messy and cluttered, and if you don't mind having a difficult time navigating the "garden" or the page.

If one is speaking of the Internet Explorer view, the same evaluation would have to be made as was made concerning the Windows experience generally. If one is speaking of the MSN Explorer wrapper, then one can give a genuine "high four" to this relatively initial entry into the field of Internet services portals. It's a high four because there are some things that do not work properly (or work in a clumsy way, like the roll over of the Favorites) in MSN Explorer and also because a logical organization of the home page is still a dream.

Microsoft Confuses Windows and the Internet

Perhaps it is because Microsoft is a relative late-comer to the Internet portal and service provision industry or to the fact that Microsoft is the developer of the Windows software, but Microsoft shows in its MSN Explorer that it is confused about the differences between Windows and the Word Wide Web.

One of the cardinal features of the Windows experience is that the software controls the user. The design of Windows is such that the user is at the mercy of whatever features the developers have designed into the product. Every pixel on the screen has a purpose. The designers and developers control where the user goes and when. For example, modal dialogs are used in the Windows environment to force a user to answer Yes, No, and sometimes Cancel before proceeding to do anything else.

The multi-tasking mode supposedly allows a user to do many things at the same time. But this is mere subterfuge because the user can have only **one** active window at a time, no matter how many other application windows are open.

The Internet, however, introduced an entirely different experience—at least until Microsoft got a hold of it. Part of the pleasure that comes with accessing the Internet is that the user can go wherever he or she wants, whenever wanted. The navigation of the Web thus differs from that of Windows. On the Web, developers give up full control of their software (and home pages). The Internet user interface is controlled in part by the developers but also by the users and the hardware and software they are using to access and display this HTML.

It appears, however, that Microsoft still thinks in Windows terms when dealing with the Internet. The Passport service is one example. This service controls who goes where and accesses what on the MSN Explorer site. Similarly, so-called personalization changes on the MSN Explorer site are immediately registered on the Microsoft servers.

Perhaps this confusion of the two media is intentional on the part of Microsoft. Perhaps this is the trend of the future. Change on the Internet is so fast, and the current state of the economy may result in changes in the way the Internet is accessed and used, with just a few dominant companies (like Microsoft and AOL) controlling how we interact with this medium. We'll see. However, I do think that those software developers who design and develop software based on what the designers and developers know or are familiar with, rather than with what the user knows and is familiar with are not doing good interface design and development—and may be doomed to eventual extinction because controlling the user in an open environment like the Web is contradictory to event-driven design.

Chapter 6

Final Evaluations

In this chapter, I want to pull together and summarize the things we've found to be wrong with Microsoft Windows, Word and MSN.

No Designer or Architect

The first and most obvious thing that is wrong with Microsoft Windows, Word, MSN, and, I suspect with all Microsoft software, is that there is no designer, no architect who marshals the forces of development into a symphony, into a coherent and intelligible structure. Much of what has been given to us over the years from Microsoft appears to have been developed by the Willy-nilly school of software architecture.

All house builders dread the mid-stream changes that homeowners are sometimes wont to make. Following a blueprint, then suddenly finding out that the owner wants changes has driven many a builder to drink. The same thing happens for software development. But starting out with a design and then changing it is one thing. In Microsoft's case, there doesn't appear to have been a blueprint, just a mess of requirements and teams of termites developing parts that were then glommed together and sent off into the world of sales. This is less true of MSN than it is of Windows, even XP, and it certainly applies to Word, which is a terrible product.

In the case of Windows, we have seen that Microsoft touts the WIMP factors (windows, icons, menus, and point and click) as the keys to the Windows experience, yet we have also seen that the icons are rife yet mostly useless and the menus excessively deep and often incoherent. The same thing can be said for Word, where the menus lack consistency and intuitive sense. It is clearly apparent that there was no "design" in the menu structures, just additive logic. And in the case of MSN, while the MSN Explorer shows some design sense, the home page that is accessible from the Explorer and any other browser lacks coherence and any design sense.

The underlying problem may be one of the paradigm or model of applications. My view is that a computer application is like a musical composition: it has to be composed with elegance and harmony—and a pleasing flow. Microsoft seems, on the other hand, to view applications as stand-alone themes—they do not fit into any harmonious or elegant "symphony"; they are just a cacophony.

The Warehouse Model

One of the features that scientists ascribe to good hypotheses about the physical universe is that they are simple and not complex. Complex and convoluted hypotheses are almost by definition false or uninformative. It is probably so in the world of software. Convoluted designs, designs that lack any sense of intuitiveness and simplicity, are probably "false" or unhelpful. Microsoft seems to be intent on making their software complex, convoluted, piling on commands (actions) to be able to be all things to all people. Yet, what we end up having is not something that is useful and a pleasure to use, but something that causes as much, if not more, pain than pleasure. This is the cardinal feature of the "warehouse" model of software design.

Instead of giving us a sleek and capable set of software in Windows, Word, and MSN, what we have is a warehouse of functions that are controlled by an oddball inventory control system (menus). Individual functions often work very well (for example, the table development functions in Word), but all of the Word functions do not work together very well in the actual process of writing, where they work at all.

User Never Considered

Another feature of Microsoft software is that despite all the ink spilled repeating the mantra of "user friendliness" and associated terms like human-centered design, the user is at the mercy of Microsoft software—rather than the other way around.

The Microsoft Developer Network (MSDN) is filled with articles describing how Microsoft is intent on responding to users and developing software that meets user expectations, but when you compare the sermon with the act, the platitudes with the reality, it is clear that Microsoft never met a user it didn't hate.

In the cases of the three applications we have looked at here, it is clear that the user is forced to do things the way Windows or Word or MSN wants things to be done. Oh, to be sure, there are some personalization features (you can change colors, items on menus, and items displayed in some cases), but none of these are designed to put the user in charge of the way the applications work.

In all three applications, though particularly in Windows, users are subjected to the invariably sudden system freeze-ups caused by things like invalid page faults, which make the system stop working. There are incompatibilities not only between Microsoft applications and other applications but also between versions of Microsoft applications; backward or forward compatibility rarely exists. The new XP release of Windows has an extensive set of "compatibility" functions to help this new system run applications that were developed for earlier versions of Windows.

Instead of putting the user in charge and fashioning applications that respond to users ways of doing their work, users are forced to do things the way the developers envision work as being done.

When problems occur, the user is often at a loss to know what to do hence an entire industry of "technical support" personnel has grown up to support users. Instead of being able to solve problems themselves, users are forced to rely upon outside "experts." Every enterprise has a technical support team to help users resolve problems in running software applications.

Microsoft has apparently never determined "who" its audience is for software development. While it talks about the "user," one is never sure which user they're talking about—the technical user or the non-technical user. Windows is simultaneously a development environment as well as a work environment. This is also true of Word, though less so of MSN Explorer. The two functions intermix. It's as if Microsoft (and, to be fair, all software developed in the industry, whether or not based on the Windows paradigm) still considers the software user to be a hobbyist who's equally at home doing things with the computer as tinkering around with them.

Microsoft has for years attempted to address this problem by releasing two versions of each release of Windows, one for the home user and one for the professional. It continues this practice with XP. But the problem remains that both the professional and home editions of XP, for example, are equally complex.

Technical and Non-technical Confused

Microsoft confuses the technical with the non-technical user. In Windows particularly, but also in Word and MSN, many tasks require expert knowledge in order to perform them.

In more recent versions of Windows, Microsoft has added "wizards" to assist users in doing things like setting up a printer or adding a new hardware peripheral, but in the great majority of cases, expert knowledge is required to make any changes in the default settings—not to mention the unexpected results of the changes and the possibility of really screwing up the OS or applications.

For example, just changing one feature of the function of a mouse requires a technical vocabulary beyond most users, and can result in dreaded consequences, which then require expert help in re-setting. It is not unheard of to need to re-install the entire OS (Windows) because of some minor change made in the Control Panel.

We also find that many of the changes that users would like to make to their application behavior requires access to and tinkering with the "Registry," the mass of system, initialization, and configuration files that can be changed at great peril. All hackers perform work with the registry files—and even experts make those changes with a sense of dread. In too many cases, changes I want (like eliminating the programs that are started up when Windows boots, and which gobble up so much memory that the system slows to a crawl) require some tinkering with registry files.

Natural and Intuitive Interface Still Lacking

One of the key intentions in creating the Windows environment Microsoft tells us is to provide the user with a natural or intuitive interface to the computer. The graphical user interface (GUI) of windows, icons, menus, and point-and-click execution was supposed to have given users a better way of manipulating and interfacing to the computer and its applications.

Icons

Instead, what we have is a proliferation of icons that have become meaningless (for the most part) and unnecessary to the interface. A few icons for the most commonly performed functions make a lot of sense, but the thousands of icons we see in applications today serve nothing more than possibly an aesthetic purpose.

The Windows "desktop" has absolutely no need for the non-intuitive icons taking up room thereon. Word is riddled with useless icons; the only icon that has any immediate and intuitive meaning for me (though it may not have universal sense because the object pictured may not be known to all possible users in the world) is the scissors icon for cut.

The MSN Explorer has some pretty icons that could just as easily have been words. As a component of the intuitive interface, icons are a hindrance and a bore. Their use should be severely curtailed in the "natural" interface.

Menus

The menus in Windows, Word, and MSN are hardly intuitive or natural.

We have seen that Windows provides menus (of commands) in its Control Panel that lack any sense of organization and intuitive intelligibility; it is difficult to find the proper menus to do what you want to do.

Word's menus are no better. You have to learn, for example, that the Tools | Options dialog is where you have to look for options related to and more suitably placed on the File, Edit, Insert, Format, Print and other menus. If you want to create and attach a template to a document, the commands related to that task are placed on several different menus, and the placement can hardly be said to be intuitive or obvious.

And the MSN home page is so cluttered and disorganized that it has nothing that could be called a logical or natural set of menus on it.

Windows

Windows themselves are hardly new. Users have always (at least since the invention of the CRT) been able to view their work within "frames" on screens, even if the early technology used scrolling screens rather than refreshed screens. I rather suspect that it is not windows that grabbed the user's attention so much as the use of colors—color CRTs did to screens what color TV did to black and white TV.

Point and Click

Only point-and-click remains as a uniquely worthwhile phenomenon. This is what allows users to manipulate applications using one hand rather than two. This is what makes the GUI most appealing—certainly not the icons or the windows or the menus. But as applied by Microsoft in its products, icons are a step backwards rather than forward, and the menus of Windows are much less intelligible and well organized than were the menus of commands provided by the pre-Windows technology.

Final Thoughts

Microsoft has been incredibly successful in marketing its software products throughout the world. There is no disputing that fact. However, the quality of their software is suspect; this book merely touches the surface of some of the problems in three of the most widely used software products from Microsoft.

The root problem is that Microsoft software lacks the touch of genius that would make its software of continuing importance. Nowhere among its products do we find a spark similar to the great simplifying genius exemplified by Einstein's famous E=MC². Nowhere do we find the use of the principle of Parsimony, that is of finding the shortest, easiest and simplest way of accomplishing some task. Microsoft's way is always the way of quantity over quality, of proliferation rather than selection, of piling on the features instead of finding a model that fits the occasion.

Doing work with Microsoft products, particularly Word, is not a natural or intuitive experience. Instead of providing tools that can be used reliably in the flow of work, Word has numerous needed functions that it does not supply, and those that it does cannot be counted upon to perform in a dependable and consistent way.

For this reason, Microsoft products will not endure the test of time. Microsoft products (like the products of probably most other software companies that currently exist) are temporary products only, products that fill a current need but cannot fulfill the promise of computing.

Somewhere down the road, if we are fortunate, a company will provide us with products of genius, products that strive for quality over quantity, products that truly help humans to do things clearly and simply with the aid of computers, products that provide tools that can be used reliably and consistently in the flow of work and that provide a natural or intuitive work environment for the user. In the meantime, we are stuck with mediocre products like the ones from Microsoft that promise but never deliver.

About the Author

Derek Kelly is retired from his fourth career as a technical writer for the software development industry. He worked initially in the mainframe environment, subsequently moving into client/server applications implemented with AIX on the servers and Windows on the clients. Though he started out with the Apple II, he has used Microsoft products ever since the IBM PC of 1981. He has published several other books including *Documenting Computer Application Systems* and *A Layman's Introduction to Robotics*. He is currently working on a book about the two major competing paradigms for software development. Derek Kelly holds a doctorate from Boston University. He lives in Aurora, Colorado. He can be reached via e-mail at andrompyx@aol.com.

Index

www.ingramcontent.com/pod-product-compliance
Lightning Source LLC
Chambersburg PA
CBHW051241050326
40689CB00007B/1024